AF361470

Academic Writing Step by Step

Frameworks for Writing
Series Editor: Martha C. Pennington,
SOAS and Birkbeck College, University of London

The series offers books focused on writing and the teaching and learning of writing in educational and real-life contexts. The hallmark of the series is the application of approaches and techniques to writing and the teaching of writing that go beyond those of English literature to draw on and integrate writing with other disciplines, areas of knowledge, and contexts of everyday life. The series entertains proposals for textbooks as well as books for teachers, teacher educators, parents, and the general public. The list includes teacher reference books and student textbooks focused on innovative pedagogy aiming to prepare teachers and students for the challenges of the twenty-first century.

Published:

The College Writing Toolkit: Tried and Tested Ideas for Teaching College Writing
Edited by Martha C. Pennington and Pauline Burton

The "Backwards" Research Guide for Writers: Using Your Life for Reflection, Connection, and Inspiration
Sonya Huber

Exploring College Writing: Reading, Writing, and Researching across the Curriculum
Dan Melzer

Tend Your Garden: Nurturing Motivation in Young Adolescent Writers
Mary Anna Kruch

Writing Poetry through the Eyes of Science: A Teacher's Guide to Scientific Literacy and Poetic Response
Nancy S. Gorrell, with Erin Colfax

Reflective Writing for Language Teachers
Thomas S. C. Farrell

Creativity and Writing Pedagogy: Linking Creative Writers, Researchers, and Teachers
Edited by Harriet Levin Millan and Martha C. Pennington

Creativity and Discovery in the University Writing Class: A Teacher's Guide
Edited by Alice Chik, Tracey Costley, and Martha C. Pennington

Academic Writing Step by Step

A Research-based Approach

Christopher N. Candlin,
Peter Crompton, and
Basil Hatim

SHEFFIELD, UK BRISTOL, CT

Published by Equinox Publishing Ltd.

UK: Office 415,
The Workstation,
15 Paternoster Row,
Sheffield,
South Yorkshire, S1 2BX

USA: ISD,
70 Enterprise Drive,
Bristol, CT 06010

www.equinoxpub.com

First published 2016

© Christopher N. Candlin, Peter Crompton, and Basil Hatim 2016

All rights reserved. No part of this publication may be reproduced or
transmitted in any form or by any means, electronic or mechanical, including
photocopying, recording or any information storage or retrieval system,
without prior permission in writing from the publishers.

British Library Cataloguing-in-Publication Data

A catalogue record for this book is available from the British Library.

ISBN   978-1-78179-057-1   (hardback)
        978-1-78179-058-8   (paperback)

Library of Congress Cataloging-in-Publication Data

Candlin, Christopher, author.
   Academic writing step by step : a research-based approach / Christopher
N. Candlin, Peter Crompton, and Basil Hatim.
     pages cm.
   Includes bibliographical references and index.
   ISBN 978-1-78179-057-1 (hb)—ISBN 978-1-78179-058-8 (pb)

1. English language—Rhetoric. 2. Academic writing. 3. Critical thinking.
4. College readers. I. Crompton, Peter, author. II. Hatim, B. (Basil), 1947–
author. III. Title.

PE1408.C29555 2015
808'.042—dc23   2014039975

Typeset by Ben Cracknell Studios | benstudios.co.uk

Printed and bound by Bell & Bain Ltd, 303 Burnfield Road, Thornliebank,
Glasgow G46 7UQ, UK, and by Lightning Source Inc. (La Vergne, TN),
Lightning Source UK Ltd. (Milton Keynes), Lightning Source AU Pty.
(Scoresby, Victoria).

CONTENTS

SERIES EDITOR'S PREFACE — IX

HOW TO USE THIS BOOK — XI

UNIT A
THE POPULARIZED RESEARCH ARTICLE — 1

UNIT B
TITLES, LEAD SUMMARIES, AND OVERVIEWS — 18

UNIT C
ARTICLE BODY AND CONCLUSION — 34

UNIT D
SUMMARIZING AND REPORTING — 52

UNIT E
THE EXPLANATORY SYNTHESIS — 70

UNIT F
THE CRITIQUE AND THE PERSUASIVE SYNTHESIS — 88

UNIT G
LOGOS, ETHOS, PATHOS, AND LOGICAL FALLACIES — 109

UNIT H
DOCUMENTATION OF SOURCES — 147

UNIT I
WHAT GOES ON INSIDE THE WRITER'S HEAD — 167

UNIT J
WHAT GOES ON INSIDE THE BEGINNER WRITER'S HEAD — 180

INDEX — 205

Professor Chris Candlin passed away during the final stages of the production of this book (in May 2015), and we would like to take this opportunity to honor his memory. Chris was a towering figure and leader in the field of applied linguistics, someone who was instrumental in building this academic hybrid and in launching a very large number of scholars and their work within its various connected disciplines. With his prodigious energy, his unending supply of original ideas, and his eye for scholarly talent in others, he was easily one of the most influential people in the field. Of the three of us, Basil knew him the longest, since Chris was the external examiner for his Ph.D. in 1981. Over the years following, Chris maintained a supportive and scholarly connection with Basil, commissioning and editing two books by him, and working with him on establishing a Ph.D. program at the Hellenic American University. Basil and Peter were delighted when Chris showed an interest in being involved in the project that has become this volume, Peter's first association with him. Martha showed a similar enthusiasm based on her nearly three-decade-long association. Martha had the pleasure of getting to know Chris in the second half of the 1980s, when she met with him at the University of Hawaii, and then at Macquarie University. From that time, Chris was a staunch supporter of Martha's work, commissioning two of her books and connecting with her frequently at conferences, meetings, and Ph.D. examinations in various countries, as well as through their mutual affiliation with the English Department at City University of Hong Kong. Chris' clarity of focus, eye for detail, creativity, and enthusiasm all made him a joy to work with: we feel great privilege at having had the opportunity to know him and to come under his influence.

Martha C. Pennington, Peter Crompton, and Basil Hatim

SERIES EDITOR'S PREFACE

Academic Writing Step by Step: A Research-based Approach is a highly original and practical writing coursebook which I am pleased to introduce as the latest addition to the Frameworks for Writing series. The book offers a compact yet comprehensive guide to academic, research-based writing in a sequence of ten self-guiding units, culminating in the writing of a research paper. The authors, Christopher N. Candlin, Peter Crompton, and Basil Hatim, have many years of experience in writing pedagogy in an international context, in addition to extensive knowledge of the research base informing this practice. With this combined background, the authors have developed a course which is authoritative as well as easy for students and teachers to use.

The approach is based on up-to-date research in discourse analysis, English for Specific Purposes, and Systemic-Functional Linguistics that has examined and characterized the features of the sorts of academic texts which involve argumentation, reporting of research, and use of sources. The authors' approach to teaching the writing of these kinds of texts is a novel one, informed by research yet simple enough for students to comprehend and learn to apply in their own work. It starts from the contrast of *given / new*, maintaining that the writer's job is to first delimit what is given, or known, about a topic and then to highlight the aspect of the topic which the writer is presenting as something new or original. The next task is then to marshal *data* to establish the new perspective and finally to develop a *conclusion* which shows how the writer's findings offer a different perspective from that of the prior research context.

Academic Writing Step by Step teaches this approach using stimulating and authentic sample texts that provide accessible, research-based discussions of issues of current interest. The book has the advantage of being relatively brief and so can fit comfortably into a one-term or one-semester writing or English course. It is designed to work on all aspects of writing, including lexical usage, grammar, organization, and referencing. It is intended especially for university undergraduates and graduate students who are speakers of English as a second or foreign language. It may be usable also as a textbook for novice writers, both ESL/EFL and first-language English speakers, at advanced secondary level (pre-university students in their last year or two of high school), who have not yet mastered the conventions of academic language and structure. I expect that students and teachers around the world will find this to be not only a useful book which they will learn much from but also a writing course which they will enjoy working through.

Martha C. Pennington
Series Editor

HOW TO USE THIS BOOK

PURPOSE

We have designed this textbook to provide ESL and EFL undergraduate and graduate students with training in how to write research papers in English. The book can be used as:

- a regular textbook for teachers or tutors and students on Academic Writing courses; or

- a stand-alone guide for students to work through on their own, with the aim of acquiring, or improving, their academic writing skills.

TIME REQUIRED

To work through the book from start to finish, and to carry out all the tasks and assignments, would occupy approximately a term in a UK or UK Commonwealth type institution, an intensive pre-sessional EAP course in such an institution, or a typical 45-class-hour semester in an American curriculum institution.

METHODOLOGY

The methodology we have designed for this the book is guided "hands on" practical discourse analysis. Each unit in the book is built around a text (a published article or part of an article) which forms the base for a sequence of learning activities requiring students to engage with the text and then carry out a writing assignment themselves.

THE GENRE OF THE TEXTS: THE POPULARIZED RESEARCH ARTICLE

Since this is a book designed to help students write research papers, most of the texts presented are popularized research articles. We believe this genre is effective and appropriate for learning research writing because:

- It is authentic, in the sense that, unlike purely pedagogic genres such as the "cause/effect" essay, it exists outside educational contexts, in authentic communicative situations.

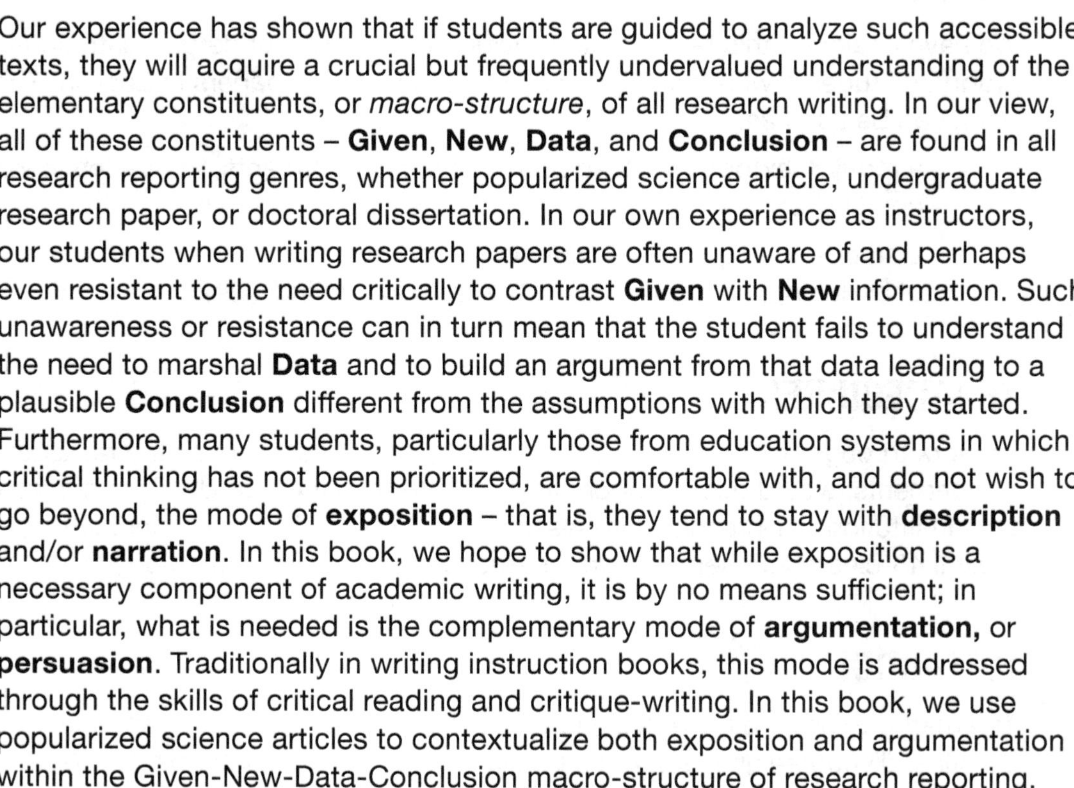

- It is accessible to laypeople, including students, being almost universally recognized in written and spoken media (e.g. in science reporting on TV and in the press).

- It can be analyzed to show precise modeling of both commonsense expectations and the rigorous scientific research method which underpin more challenging academic writing genres (e.g. theses and academic journal articles).

Our experience has shown that if students are guided to analyze such accessible texts, they will acquire a crucial but frequently undervalued understanding of the elementary constituents, or *macro-structure*, of all research writing. In our view, all of these constituents – **Given**, **New**, **Data**, and **Conclusion** – are found in all research reporting genres, whether popularized science article, undergraduate research paper, or doctoral dissertation. In our own experience as instructors, our students when writing research papers are often unaware of and perhaps even resistant to the need critically to contrast **Given** with **New** information. Such unawareness or resistance can in turn mean that the student fails to understand the need to marshal **Data** and to build an argument from that data leading to a plausible **Conclusion** different from the assumptions with which they started. Furthermore, many students, particularly those from education systems in which critical thinking has not been prioritized, are comfortable with, and do not wish to go beyond, the mode of **exposition** – that is, they tend to stay with **description** and/or **narration**. In this book, we hope to show that while exposition is a necessary component of academic writing, it is by no means sufficient; in particular, what is needed is the complementary mode of **argumentation,** or **persuasion**. Traditionally in writing instruction books, this mode is addressed through the skills of critical reading and critique-writing. In this book, we use popularized science articles to contextualize both exposition and argumentation within the Given-New-Data-Conclusion macro-structure of research reporting.

TOPICS OF THE TEXTS

The texts are intended to illustrate the research reporting macro-structure that is common across a range of academic disciplines. We have selected texts which describe a range of engaging academic research topics that are related to everyday life.

FORMAT OF THE UNITS

The units follow a common format, and most contain the following components:

Section	Content
Unit Focus	A bulleted list of key text-organizing concepts covered in the unit
Context	Questions designed to help orient students to the context and the content of the research described in the example text
Words in Context	Explanations of selected vocabulary used in the text *Students are encouraged to make sure they understand each word in bold before tackling the text.*
The Text	The whole text in an authentic format, followed by questions on each section separately *Students should first skim through the text and then answer the questions.*
Did You Get That?	Answers to the questions, with commentary
Grammar in Context	Explanations of selected grammar points illustrated in the text *Students may test their understanding of the points in tasks provided.*
Text Organization	Explanations of text-organizing patterns illustrated in the text *Students may test their understanding of the patterns in tasks provided.*
How To	A bulleted list of the key text-organizing concepts, framed in terms of the students' own writing needs
Assignment	An extended writing task designed to give students practice in employing the unit's key text-organizing concepts for themselves

At the end of the book, there is an index of of key concepts to help teacher and student monitor their understanding of the concepts.

PROGRESSION

As the key concepts are progressively introduced and developed, the writing assignments become more complex, concluding (in Unit J) with an analysis of the development over three drafts of an example student research paper.

THE POPULARIZED RESEARCH ARTICLE

UNIT FOCUS

In this Unit, you will be able to see:

- What a Popularized Research Article looks like "from above," that is, its macro-structure on a global level;

- How the various components of such an article are put together:
  - **Title** and **Lead Summary**
  - **Overview**
  - Review of commonly held but questionable assumptions – the **Given**
  - Presentation of research supporting the new proposal – the **New**
  - **Conclusion**

CONTEXT

In each unit of this book, you will be working with an authentic text. The text in this unit is an article about some new research on whether sick animals can treat themselves (medically). To prepare for reading the text, answer the questions below.

1. What do you think most people believe?

    (a) Animals can treat themselves.

    (b) Animals cannot treat themselves.

2. Let us assume that most people believe (b), animals cannot treat themselves. What kind of evidence would we need to convince them of (a)?

    (a) Observations by naturalists of sick animals eating unusual substances and becoming healthy again.

    (b) Statistics which show how huge numbers of animals die from illness.

WORDS IN CONTEXT

Before you read the text, doing some preparatory work on useful vocabulary is going to help. Below we have highlighted in **bold** some words in the text that you may not know and added explanations in *italics*.

Using a dictionary if necessary, make sure you understand each word in bold and check the box on the right before moving to the next highlighted word.

animals **wrinkle** (*pull up*) their noses when eating food they don't like	☐
vomited (*threw up*) on the carpet after eating some bad food	☐
when my soccer team lost the final I felt **"as sick as a parrot"** (*very disappointed*)	☐
self-medicating behavior (*when people or animals treat themselves for illness*)	☐
collating (*collecting*) examples of animals treating themselves	☐
they consume dirt – a behavior known as **geophagy** (*earth-eating*)	☐
But **animal behaviorists** (*scientists studying animal behavior*) are now more keen on the idea	☐
mechanical scours (*cleaning by rubbing rather than using chemicals*)	☐

THE TEXT

Now you are ready to read the text.

a. First, skim through the whole text to get the general idea (or gist) of what the text is about.

b. Then read the text as broken down into sections, answering the questions. (Some multiple-choice items may have more than one correct answer.)

Animal Doctors

Many animals seem able to treat their illnesses themselves. Humans may have a thing or two to learn from them.

When Cindy Engel notices that her cat, Darwin, has vomited on her carpet, she doesn't worry…

For the past decade Dr Engel, a lecturer in environmental sciences at Britain's Open University, has been collating examples of self-medicating behavior in wild animals. She recently published a book* on the subject. In a talk at the Edinburgh Science Festival earlier this month, she explained that the idea that animals can treat themselves has been regarded with some scepticism by her colleagues in the past. But a growing number of animal behaviorists now think that wild animals can and do deal with their own medical needs.

…

A third instance of animal self-medication is the use of mechanical scours to get rid of gut parasites. In 1972 Richard Wrangham, a researcher at the Gombe Stream Reserve in Tanzania, noticed that chimpanzees were eating the leaves of a tree called *Aspilia*. The chimps chose the leaves carefully by testing them in their mouths. Having chosen a leaf, a chimp would fold it into a fan and swallow it. Some of the chimps were noticed wrinkling their noses as they swallowed these leaves, suggesting the experience was unpleasant. Later, undigested leaves were found on the forest floor.

Following [these observations], Dr Engel is now particularly excited about how knowledge of the way that animals look after themselves could be used to improve the health of livestock. People might also be able to learn a thing or two—and may, indeed, already have done so. Geophagy, for example, is a common behavior in many parts of the world. The medical stalls in African markets frequently sell tablets made of different sorts of clays, appropriate to different medical conditions….

Dirt can sometimes be good for you, and to be "as sick as a parrot" may, after all, be a state to be desired.

* *Wild Health*. Weidenfeld and Nicolson, London; 276 pages.

[*The Economist*, April 18, 2002]

[A]

Animal Doctors

Many animals seem able to treat their illnesses themselves. Humans may have a thing or two to learn from them.

Section A is primarily intended to
(a) conclude the article.
(b) present research supporting a new position.
(c) review commonly held but questionable assumptions.
(d) provide an overview.
(e) attract the reader and summarize the article.

[B]

When Cindy Engel notices that her cat, Darwin, has vomited on her carpet, she doesn't worry…

For the past decade Dr Engel, a lecturer in environmental sciences at Britain's Open University, has been collating examples of self-medicating behavior in wild animals. She recently published a book* on the subject. In a talk at the Edinburgh Science Festival earlier this month, she explained that the idea that animals can treat themselves has been regarded with some scepticism by her colleagues in the past. But a growing number of animal behaviorists now think that wild animals can and do deal with their own medical needs.

Section B is primarily intended to
(a) conclude the article.
(b) present research supporting a new position.
(c) review commonly held but questionable assumptions.
(d) provide an overview.
(e) attract the reader and summarize the article.

The underlined sentence of Section B is primarily intended to
(a) conclude the article.
(b) present research supporting a new position.
(c) review commonly held but questionable assumptions.
(d) provide an overview.
(e) attract the reader and summarize the article.

[C] A third instance of animal self-medication is the use of mechanical scours to get rid of gut parasites. In 1972 Richard Wrangham, a researcher at the Gombe Stream Reserve in Tanzania, noticed that chimpanzees were eating the leaves of a tree called *Aspilia*. The chimps chose the leaves carefully by testing them in their mouths. Having chosen a leaf, a chimp would fold it into a fan and swallow it. Some of the chimps were noticed wrinkling their noses as they swallowed these leaves, suggesting the experience was unpleasant. Later, undigested leaves were found on the forest floor.

Section C is primarily intended to
(a) conclude the article.
(b) present research supporting a new position.
(c) review commonly held but questionable assumptions.
(d) provide an overview.
(e) attract the reader and summarize the article.

[D] Following [these observations], Dr Engel is now particularly excited about how knowledge of the way that animals look after themselves could be used to improve the health of livestock. People might also be able to learn a thing or two—and may, indeed, already have done so. Geophagy, for example, is a common behavior in many parts of the world. The medical stalls in African markets frequently sell tablets made of different sorts of clays, appropriate to different medical conditions....

Dirt can sometimes be good for you, and to be "as sick as a parrot" may, after all, be a state to be desired.

Section D is primarily intended to
(a) conclude the article.
(b) present research supporting a new position.
(c) review commonly held but questionable assumptions.
(d) provide an overview.
(e) attract the reader and summarize the article.

DID YOU GET THAT?

Here we present answers to the questions we asked above.

Check the boxes below if you got the right answers.

[A]

☐ (e) attract the reader and summarize the article.

Note: We call the part after the title the **Lead Summary**.

[B]

☐ (d) provide an overview.

☐ **Underlined sentence:** (c) review commonly held but questionable assumptions.

[C]

☐ (b) present research supporting a new position.

[D]

☐ (a) conclude the article.

GRAMMAR IN CONTEXT

1. Using Modal Verbs to indicate degrees of certainty

Look at the verbs in bold in the sentences in the first and second columns below. Notice how the verbs *may, can, could* in the second column qualify the meaning of the verbs which follow them. These qualifying verbs are called **modal verbs**. We show each sentence *without* the modal verb in the first column. In these examples, modal verbs make the sentences either more **certain** or more **possible**. Because research scientists want to find out what is possible and what is certain, modal verbs are common in research writing.

Statement without Modal Verb	Statement with Modal Verb	Meaning of Modal Verb
Humans **have** a thing or two to learn from them.	Humans **may have** a thing or two to learn from them.	We don't know for sure, but it is possible that the statement is true.
Dirt **is** sometimes good for you…	Dirt **can** sometimes be good for you…	The statement is not always true but it is possible.
…how knowledge of the way that animals look after themselves **is used** to improve the health of livestock.	…how knowledge of the way that animals look after themselves **could be used** to improve the health of livestock.	The statement may not happen – or come true – in the future, but it is possible.

☑ TASK 1

From the context, what would be an appropriate modal verb to include in the following sentences?

We have done the first example for you.

1. Nearly all living things perish at such pressures. In special circumstances, however, some species ______can______ survive.

2. When magnesium and sodium burn, they oxidize and become heavier. Potassium is a similar element so after burning it _______________ become heavier too.

3. Most cars have to be scrapped before 200,000 miles, but occasionally you _______________ find one of these older cars worth driving.

4. What caused the last ice age isn't known for certain. It _______________ have been a meteorite strike.

5. Numbers of unemployed have fallen considerably in the last year. This drop _______________ affect attitudes towards rising immigration figures.

2. How to be cautious in what you write: The importance of Hedging

Apart from using modal verbs, there are other ways in which researchers show that their statements are not drawn from direct observations, or are not definite.

Statement without Hedging	Statement with Hedging	Meaning of Hedging
Many animals **are** able to treat their illnesses themselves.	Many animals **seem** able to treat their illnesses themselves.	Appearance/Deduction
Not all animals **are** as smart as chimps.	It **seems** that not all animals are as smart as chimps.	The statement appears to be true, but the author does not want to be definite about it.
…**showing** that the experience was unpleasant.	…**suggesting** that the experience was unpleasant.	

Using modal verbs and expressions like those in the above examples is called **Hedging.** To see why people hedge, imagine you have a friend called Sam, who comes to college in a red Ferrari. At college someone asks you if Sam is here today. You have not actually seen Sam, but you look out of the window to the parking lot and see a red Ferrari. You might well answer:

He seems to be here.

or

I think he's here because there's his red Ferrari.

You hedge what you say because you have not actually seen Sam at college today. Maybe there are other explanations for the red Ferrari in the lot (e.g. it might not be Sam's car, or another student might be borrowing Sam's car today). In the same way, when they write, researchers use hedging to show that their statements are not based on certain knowledge but on reasoning from the evidence which they have.

☑ TASK 2

Now we would like you to rewrite the sentences below, using a modal verb to hedge what you are writing. In each case the purpose of hedging the verb is to make clear to the reader that the sentence is not a statement of fact, but a deduction based on evidence. The evidence on which the deductions are based is given in brackets.

We have done the first example for you.

1. **Animals that have been reared in zoos do not survive if released into the wild.**
   [In some cases such animals have died within weeks.]

Animals that have been reared in zoos may not survive if released into the wild.

2. **In the next decade 3D printers will be as common as color printers are today.**
   [Futurologists predict this.]

3. **Twenty years ago, students used libraries more than students today.**
   [If library withdrawal records then and now are compared, there are a lot fewer loans these days.]

4. **Microwave radiation from cell phones causes cancer.**
   [1% of laboratory rats exposed to it developed cancer.]

5. **Tyrannosaurus Rex dinosaurs ate smaller dinosaurs.**
   [Newly found fossilized T-Rex teeth look like those of carnivores today.]

TEXT ORGANIZATION

Here we invite you to think about and practice some important features of academic writing above the level of words and sentences. The focus is on how texts are organized.

Given and New in writing student research papers

In the "Animal Doctors" text, the writer takes a problematic assumption (*Animals cannot treat themselves*) and offers a correction (*Animals can treat themselves*). In this book, we call such a problematic assumption the **Given** and its correction the **New**. All research writing depends on contrasting the Given with the New in this sense.

☑ TASK 3

To identify possible Givens for a topic, ask yourself *What does everyone already know and accept about the topic? How do people commonly view this topic?* Try to come up with Givens for the topics below. We have supplied one example of a Given for each topic.

Globalization

Improved international communication exposes people to other cultures.

Social networking sites

The younger generation spends a lot of time and energy communicating with peers on social network sites.

TV violence

There is a lot more realistically portrayed violence on TV these days than there was in the past.

Unhappy childhood

People who have had an unhappy childhood are emotionally handicapped.

Shopping malls

Shopping malls encourage and facilitate materialism and consumerism.

Understanding the contrast between Given and New will help you decide on good topics for the research papers your professors ask you to write. Some topics are simply unsuitable for research because there is in fact no Given/New contrast. For example, *Diseases caused by smoking* is unlikely to be a suitable topic unless you can find new research which calls into question what is now widely regarded as a fact, that *smoking cigarettes causes cancer and heart and lung disease*. If you can't find any New element in your topic, it is almost certainly **not** a good topic for research.

☑ TASK 4

Now see if you can brainstorm ideas to put a New slant on these same topics. What sort of evidence and conclusions could you use to surprise your readers in the paper? What goes against what people might naturally expect? These are likely to be the interesting things to focus on.

Globalization

has impoverished our souls

people have become materialistic and superficial

Social networking sites

TV violence

Unhappy childhood

Shopping malls

Awareness

☑ TASK 5

Read the following segments drawn from different articles. Each segment represents one of the components of an academic article as listed on the left below, with their functions shown in the list on the right. See if you can identify the components illustrated in items 1–5 and label them, using the correct term for each one:

Component	Function
Title and **Lead Summary**	Attracts the reader and summarizes the article
Overview	Provides an overview
Given	Presents commonly held but questionable assumptions
New	Presents research supporting a new position
Conclusion	Closes article

We have included the first label for you.

[1]
Chickens are capable of feeling empathy, scientists believe

Domestic chickens display signs of empathy, the ability to "feel another's pain" that is at the heart of compassion, a study has found.

Component: _Title and Lead Summary_

[2] No, your pet dog is not likely ever to catch on fire, so what are flame retardants doing in domestic canines? Indiana University researchers found manmade flame retardants in the blood of pet dogs at levels five to ten times greater than those found in humans. A previous study found even higher levels in cats.

Component: _______________________________

[3] "Coffee drinkers should rejoice," said Dr. Sharonne N. Hayes, a cardiologist at Mayo Clinic, responding to the study. "Coffee is often made out to be potentially bad for your heart. There really hasn't been any study that convincingly said coffee is bad."

Component: _______________________________

[4] Other observations also support the idea that clay is detoxifying. Towards the tropics the amount of toxic compounds in plants increases – and so does the amount of earth eaten by herbivores. Elephants lick clay from mud holes all year round, except in September when they are bingeing on fruit which, because it has evolved to be eaten, is not toxic. And the addition of clay to the diets of domestic cattle increases the amount of nutrients that they can absorb from their food by 10–20%.

Component: ____

[5] In the historical debate between mind and matter, mind won and silenced the voice of the body; it interpreted the body in terms of mind and considered it a mute machine that only reason could discover. It is time to recover that corporeal voice, to recast the Epicurean thinking that puts pleasure in the place of thought, that imagines bodily pleasure to be a kind of thinking. Good health will then be understood as a consequence of good pleasure, and adult pleasure will be prized, not tabooed; moderated, not censored; indulged, not feared.

Component: ____

☑ TASK 6

The components you have identified above all appear in the "Animal Doctors" text also. For each of the components below (A–E), find one or two sentences (word for word) from the "Animal Doctors" text which belong to that component. When combined these sentences should form a Summary of the whole text.

We have done Component A for you.

[A] **Lead Summary** Many animals seem able to treat their illnesses themselves.

[B] **Overview**

____

____

____

[C] **The Given (assumption being questioned)**

....

....

....

[D] **The New proposal**

....

....

....

[E] **Conclusion**

....

....

....

How To

Write a Paper

Make sure that your paper has the following elements:

- An eye-catching and informative **Title**
- A **Lead Summary** which serves as a preview of the paper
- An **Overview**
- A **Body** (see Unit C) presenting the **Given** and relevant evidence for the **New**
- An overall **Conclusion**

ASSIGNMENT

In order to consolidate your understanding of the five elements, write a Summary of "Animal Doctors" which includes all five elements in the order shown above. Try to use two or three sentences to do justice to each element. Use mainly your own words but include quotations where appropriate.

The Summary should be 200–300 words.

We have done the first element, the Title and Lead Summary, for you.

1. Title and Lead Summary

Animals Use Nature To Heal Themselves

Animals wounded in the wild or stricken by disease possess a remarkable

ability to treat their ailments. This has important implications for humans.

2. Overview

3. Body: Given

4. Body: New

5. Conclusion

TITLES, LEAD SUMMARIES, AND OVERVIEWS

UNIT FOCUS

In this Unit, you will be able to see:

- How writers develop **Titles**, **Lead Summaries**, and **Overviews** in popularized research articles;

- How these components function and work together in the overall structure of an article;

- How the relationship between the **Given** (a problematic assumption) and the **New** (the proposed position) is crucial in developing the Title, the Lead Summary, and the Overview in research articles.

CONTEXT

1. Imagine an article with the title "Dolphins should be treated as 'persons'." What do you think prompted the writer to write the article?

   (a) A situation that is satisfactory and acceptable.

   (b) An assumption that is problematic, even though it is commonly held.

2. If the problem is to do with people's indifference regarding the status of dolphins, what would you expect to be New in such an article?

   (a) Dolphins are animals and that's all there is to it.

   (b) Dolphins are not exactly *animals* and should be treated as a separate kind of "person."

3. How could you back up the New proposition? What evidence would persuade you to treat dolphins as "persons"?

    (a) Observing and documenting what dolphins do similarly to other animals.

    (b) Observing and documenting what dolphins do similarly to human beings.

4. What kind of conclusion do you think the writer is likely to reach?

5. Since we are focusing in this Unit on article Titles, Lead Summaries, and Overviews, what do you think makes these components particularly effective?

    (a) They announce the topic accurately.

    (b) The way the writer presents the Given assumption and the New position in an accurate, vivid, and witty manner.

Note that this text (and some others in this book) has some words in British spelling (*recognised*, *behavioural*, *behaviour*) and British punctuation (single rather than double quotes).

WORDS IN CONTEXT

Using a dictionary if necessary, make sure you understand each word in bold and check the box before moving to the next item.

Dolphins have been **declared** (*announced; claimed to be*) the world's second most intelligent species	☐
Dolphins have been **recognised** (*agreed by experts*) as very clever animals	☐
a series of **behavioural** studies (*examining animal behavior*)	☐
bright (*intelligent*)	☐
inspect (*examine*) various parts of their bodies	☐
can learn a **rudimentary** (*elementary; basic*) language	☐
symbol-based language (*using visual cues, not words*)	☐
with a strong **sense of self** (*acting as an individual*)	☐
"cultural" animals (*animals that can socialize and learn from each other*)	☐

THE TEXT

Now you are ready to read the text.

a. First, skim through the whole text to get the general idea (or gist) of what the text is about.

b. Then read the text as broken down into sections, answering the questions. (Some multiple-choice items may have more than one correct answer.)

Dolphins should be treated as "non-human persons"

Dolphins have been <u>declared</u> the world's second most intelligent creatures after humans, with scientists <u>suggesting</u> they are so bright that they should be treated as "non-human persons".

Dolphins have long been recognised as among the most intelligent of animals but many researchers had placed them below chimps, which some studies have found can reach the intelligence levels of three-year-old children. **Recently, however,** a series of behavioural studies has suggested that dolphins, especially species such as the bottlenose, could be the brighter of the two. The studies show how dolphins have distinct personalities, a strong sense of self and can think about the future.

It has also become clear that they are "cultural" animals, meaning that new types of behaviour can quickly be picked up by one dolphin from another. In one study, Diana Reiss, professor of psychology at Hunter College, City University of New York, showed that bottlenose dolphins could recognise themselves in a mirror and use it to inspect various parts of their bodies, an ability that had been thought limited to humans and great apes. In another, she found that captive animals also had the ability to learn a rudimentary symbol-based language.

(Jonathan Leake, *Sunday Times* (London), 31 October 2010)

[A]

Dolphins should be treated as "non-human persons"

The Title is striking because
(a) the content is factual.
(b) the words are decorative.
(c) the idea that there are "persons" who are "non-human" arouses curiosity.

[B]

Dolphins have been <u>declared</u> the world's second most intelligent creatures after humans, with scientists <u>suggesting</u> they are so bright that they should be treated as "non-human persons".

In the Lead Summary, the words *declared* and *suggesting* indicate
(a) the Given but erroneous assumption that dolphins are only animals.
(b) the New position that dolphins are not just animals.

[C]

Dolphins have long been recognised as among the most intelligent of animals but many researchers had placed them below chimps, which some studies have found can reach the intelligence levels of three-year-old children. **Recently, however,** a series of behavioural studies has suggested that dolphins, especially species such as the bottlenose, could be the brighter of the two. The studies show how dolphins have distinct personalities, a strong sense of self and can think about the future.

What is the function and relevance of the initial sentence in the Overview (underlined)?
(a) It is a story with a moral lesson.
(b) It is a quote.
(c) It is a statement of the New position to be adopted in the article (*dolphins are cleverer than chimps*).
(d) It is a statement of the Given position to be questioned in the article (*dolphins are not as clever as chimps*).

***Recently, however,* signals**
(a) Given assumption to be questioned (*dolphins are not as smart as chimps*).
(b) New proposal to be put forward (*dolphins are smarter than chimps*).

> **[D]** It has also become clear that they are "cultural" animals, meaning that new types of behaviour can quickly be picked up by one dolphin from another. In one study, Diana Reiss, professor of psychology at Hunter College, City University of New York, showed that bottlenose dolphins could recognise themselves in a mirror and use it to inspect various parts of their bodies, an ability that had been thought limited to humans and great apes. In another, she found that captive animals also had the ability to learn a rudimentary symbol-based language.

This section is no longer part of the Overview, because it
(a) is a memorable quote.
(b) is an entertaining anecdote.
(c) merely hints at the New position (*dolphins should be treated as persons*).
(d) documents the New position in precise terms.

DID YOU GET THAT?

Check the boxes below if you got the right answers.

[A] – Title

☐ (c) the idea that there are "persons" who are "non-human" arouses curiosity.

[B] – Lead Summary

☐ (b) the New position that dolphins are not just animals.

[C] – Overview

☐ **underlined sentence**: (d) It is a statement of the Given position to be questioned in the article (*dolphins are not as clever as chimps*).

☐ ***Recently, however***: (b) New proposal to be put forward (*dolphins are smarter than chimps*).

[D] – Body

☐ (d) documents the New position in precise terms – in particular, evidence that dolphins are slightly more than animals.

☑ TASK 1

Complete the sentences below to produce a four-sentence summary of the article without repeating its exact wording.

Scientists have known for a long time that

Recently, however, some scientists have discovered that

The experiments they carried out basically

Their conclusion is that

☑ TASK 1

GRAMMAR IN CONTEXT

1. The Present Perfect: Emphasizing time related to the present, of current relevance

Notice the specific meaning of the present perfect tense in the examples below. Whereas the simple past tense presents a past event or state of affairs, the present perfect connects past and present by emphasizing the current relevance of information.

Simple Past	Present Perfect	Meaning of Present Perfect
Dolphins **were** declared the world's second most intelligent creatures…	Dolphins **have been declared** the world's second most intelligent creatures…	The declaration is recent.
Dolphins **were** long **recognised** as among the most intelligent of animals…	Dolphins **have** long **been recognised** as among the most intelligent of animals…	This event happened in the past but continues to be relevant now and there is more to say about it.
Recently, however, a series of behavioural studies **suggested** that dolphins…	Recently, however, a series of behavioural studies **has suggested** that dolphins…	These recent studies provide relevant background for the author's points.
It also **became** clear that they are "cultural" animals…	It **has** also **become** clear that they are "cultural" animals…	This is a recent finding that connects to the author's points.

☑ TASK 2

From the context in each sentence, try to decide whether the information below has *current relevance.* Should the verbs be in the simple past or the present perfect?
Circle the appropriate form.

We have done the first example for you.

1. Einstein was working in a patent office when he **[wrote / has written]** a paper on the Special Theory of Relativity.

2. I started my book last October but **[didn't finish / haven't finished]** it yet.

3. The recent discovery of the Higgs Boson particle **[changed / has changed]** the way particle physics textbooks will need to be written.

4. Stephen Hawking **[graduated / has graduated]** from Cambridge University in 1961.

5. The possible applications of the discovery of the human genome **[were not exploited / have not been exploited]** fully yet.

6. There **[were / have been]** no manned lunar landings since the Apollo missions ended.

2. The Past Perfect: Emphasizing time related to a time farther back in the past

Notice the specific meaning of the past perfect tense in the examples below. The past perfect tense indicates an event or state of affairs which occurred farther back in the past than another past event or state of affairs.

Simple Past	Past Perfect	Meaning of Past Perfect
Dolphins have long been recognised as among the most intelligent of animals, but many researchers **placed** them below chimps…	Dolphins have long been recognised as among the most intelligent of animals, but many researchers **had placed** them below chimps…	This event or state existed at an earlier stage in the past than the one currently being reported.
Diana Reiss…showed that bottlenose dolphins could recognise themselves in a mirror, … an ability that **was thought** limited to humans and great apes.	Diana Reiss…showed that bottlenose dolphins could recognise themselves in a mirror, … an ability that **had been thought** limited to humans and great apes.	

☑ TASK 3

Now try to combine the following pairs of sentences. Change one of the verbs into the past perfect to show the relationship between the two situations described.

We have done the first example for you.

1. **Al-Ghazali wrote seventeen books. He was working on another one when he died, in 1111.**

When he died, in 1111, Al-Ghazali ____ had written ____ seventeen books and was working on another.

2. **Scholars thought that the sun went round the earth. Galileo proved the opposite.**

Before Galileo proved the opposite, scholars ________________ that the sun went round the earth.

3. **Scientists believed that language almost completely governed how young people think. The results of a 2010 experiment suggested the scientists were wrong.**

The results of a 2010 experiment suggested that even after youngsters learn language, it does not govern their thinking as much as scientists ________________ .

4. **Some archaeologists believed Yax K'uk Mo came from Teotihuacn, in the Mexican highlands. In 2000, analysis of Yax K'uk Mo's newly discovered tomb revealed that he was born much closer to Copn.**

Before analysis of his newly discovered tomb in 2000 revealed that he was born much closer to Copn, some archaeologists ___________________ Yax K'uk Mo came from Teotihuacn, in the Mexican highlands.

5. **Research published last year showed that the moon's magnetic field lasted for more than 400 million years. Before this research scientists thought such a small object could not be magnetized for so long.**

Until research published last year showed that the moon's magnetic field lasted for more than 400 million years, scientists ___________________ such a small object could not be magnetized for so long.

6. **In the twentieth century, people's capacity to detect detail in peripheral vision was assumed to be very limited. Research on US Navy pilots a decade ago showed that in fact people could detect a lot.**

Research on US Navy pilots a decade ago demonstrated people's capacity to detect far more detail in peripheral vision than ___________________.

TEXT ORGANIZATION

Given and New contrast in Title, Lead Summary, and Overview

Here we invite you to notice how the Given and New contrast is threaded through the Title, Lead Summary, and Overview. The use of the modal verb "should" in both the Title and Lead Summary highlights the scientists' New position. It makes a contrast with the Given, which is implicit and not stated – *Dolphins are not now treated as "non-human persons."* In the Overview, the word *Recently* first presents the New and then introduces the body of the article. This gives details of the data which led the scientists to their New position.

Following the Title and Lead Summary, an Overview performs several functions. Ideally, an Overview

- Gets attention
- Sets the scene
- States the Given
- States the New
- Offers a map or sketch of the article

☑ TASK 4

In the text of the Overview in the article in this unit, two functions are missing. Try to add sentences which provide these functions.

1. Attention-getting scene-setter (anecdote, provocative question, etc.)

-----

2. Given

Many researchers had placed dolphins below chimps,

-----

3. New

Dolphins could be the brighter of the two

-----

4. Map

Awareness

☑ **TASK 5**

Read the following segments drawn from different articles. For the Title, Lead Summary, and Overview in each segment, underline what you think is the New information. Write in the space provided what you think is the Given which is being questioned. We have done the first one for you.

1

Cats outsmarted in psychologist's test

Cats are not stupid, they're just different. Strings experiment shows limits of feline intelligence.

It will cause outrage among some cat owners, but research suggests the pets are not as clever as some humans assumed – or at least they think in a way we have yet to fathom.

Psychology lecturer Britta Osthaus says cats do not understand cause-and-effect connections between objects. She tested the thought processes of 15 of them by attaching fish and biscuit treats to one end of a piece of string, placing them under a plastic screen to make them unreachable and...

[James Meikle, *The Guardian*, June 16, 2009]

Given: _Cats are clever in the way humans are._

2

The Case Against Health

Why pleasure is our highest good.

In the United States, health has become a commodity and an industry. We spend vastly more than any other country on health care, and increasingly our health is our wealth. Even in our down economy, health-care spending continues to grow. In 2006, Americans spent about $35-billion on diets and diet services, in large part under the illusion that they were improving their health. Yet we consistently fall behind Britain, not to mention France, in every measure of public health. Some place American public health just ahead of that of Slovenia...

[Excerpted from article by Dr. Richard Klein, *The Chronicle Review*, *The Chronicle of Higher Education*, 21 November 2010; picture credit Marc Yankus]

Given:

3

Love of musical harmony is not nature but nurture

Music appreciation, once thought to be determined by the physical properties of our ear, is more a function of training and education, says Neil McLachlan from the Melbourne School of Psychological Sciences.

Our love of music and appreciation of musical harmony is learnt and not based on natural ability, a new study by University of Melbourne researchers has found. Associate Professor Neil McLachlan from the Melbourne School of Psychological Sciences said previous theories about how we appreciate music were based on the physical properties of sound, the ear itself and an innate ability to hear harmony.

"Our study shows that musical harmony can be learnt and it is a matter of training the brain to hear the sounds," Associate Professor McLachlan said…

[*Science Daily*, 14 February 2013]

Given: ____

4

DNA study shows Europeans share common ancestors who lived 1,000 years ago

Europeans appear to be more closely related than previously thought.

Scientists who compared DNA samples from people in different parts of the continent found that most had common ancestors living just 1,000 years ago.

The results confirm decade-old mathematical models, but will nevertheless come as a surprise to Europeans accustomed to thinking of ancient nations composed of distinct ethnic groups like "Germans," "Irish" or "Serbs."

"What's remarkable about this is how closely everyone is related to each other," said Graham Coop of the University of California, Davis, who co-wrote the study published Tuesday in the journal PLoS Biology…

[*Associated Press*, May 8, 2013]

Given: ____

How To

Write a Title, a Lead Summary, and an Overview

Make sure that your paper has the following elements:

- An eye-catching and informative **Title** which

  - hints at the questionable **Given** position;

  and/or

  - indicates the **New** position you want to highlight.

- A **Lead Summary** which uses vivid language to attract the reader's attention to

  - the **Given** position you want to question;

  and

  - the **New** position you want to highlight.

- An **Overview** which

  - sets the scene (perhaps by using an anecdote, a quote or a global statement of the issues);
  - re-states the **Given** and the **New** as a Research Question;
  - briefly tells the reader about the kind of evidence (e.g. data) your paper will present to support the **New** position;
  - helps the reader navigate a way through your paper by giving a map;
  - anticipates the **Conclusion** your paper will reach.

ASSIGNMENT

We list below the possible research paper topics you considered in Unit A:

Globalization

Social networking sites

TV violence

Unhappy childhood

Shopping malls

Now choose one of these topics and compose a Title, a Lead Summary, and an Overview for a paper on the topic, following the guidelines we provide above. Keep to the word limits shown.

Title   (5–10 words)

Lead Summary   (20–30 words)

Overview   (100–150 words)

ARTICLE BODY AND CONCLUSION

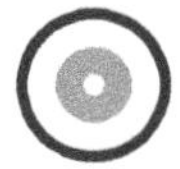

UNIT FOCUS

In this Unit, you will be able to see:

- How the **Body** of the Popularized Research Article is developed as a **Given–New** structure, or more simply, **Problem–Solution** structure;

- How the questionable **Given** assumptions are presented as background to the **New** proposals in the research article;

- How the **Conclusion** is presented.

The Given and New form the core of what is referred to as a **Thesis Statement**. This is normally the answer to a **Research Question**.

For example, if your Research Question in an article you plan to write is "Can animals treat themselves?", the Thesis Statement will be something like "It is possible for animals to treat themselves."

In terms of Given and New, the Given here is "Animals cannot treat themselves," and the New is "Yes, they can!"

CONTEXT

1. Think about the following statement: "A good night's sleep after studying helps you remember what you have studied." If you asked your friends or family about this claim, do you think they would

   (a) Agree?

   (b) Disagree?

2. Why do you think there could be a general agreement that "a good night's sleep is necessary for a good performance in a test the following day"?

3. If we were to carry out some good research on this issue, what do you think it would show?

   (a) Sleep has no effect on whether or not you remember information.

(b) Sleep helps you remember information, provided that you know you'll need the information.

4. For the sake of argument, let's assume that research found answer (b) above to be true. What kind of data (evidence, examples) do you think would support answer (b)?

   (a) Comparing the pop quiz results of a group of students with data on how much each student slept the night before.

   (b) Comparing the quiz results of two groups of students, one taking an announced, scheduled quiz, the other taking an unannounced, pop quiz.

5. Assuming that (b) is the correct answer, which of the following is the more plausible Conclusion for the research?

   (a) Sleep helps you remember information provided that you know what you need the information for.

   (b) Remembering information is not affected by how much sleep you have had.

WORDS IN CONTEXT

Using a dictionary if necessary, make sure you understand each word in bold and check the box before moving to the next item.

to cement (*firmly establish*) the day's memories	☐
Sleep improved **retention** (*remembering*)	☐
sleep benefits its **consolidation** (*firm establishment*)	☐
from **short-term** (*temporary*) storage into **long-term** (*more lasting*) holding	☐
it's not **automatic** (*it does not happen by itself*)	☐
to **reactivate** (*bring back; make active again*) old memories	☐
A night of z's (*deep, comfortable sleep*)	☐
eight hours of **shut-eye** (*sleep*)	☐
if you **explicitly** (*consciously*) tell yourself	☐
Concentration-type game (*in which your mind is focused*)	☐
In an **elegant** (*neat, comprehensive, top-quality*) series of experiments	☐

THE TEXT

Now you are ready to read the text.

a. First, skim through the whole text to get the general idea (or gist) of what the text is about.

b. Then read the text as broken down into sections, answering the questions. (Some multiple-choice items may have more than one correct answer.)

Sleep Your Way to An "A"

Getting a good night's sleep has long been known to cement the day's memories, moving them from short-term storage into long-term holding, but new research shows that it's not automatic

Getting a good night's sleep **has long been known** to cement the day's memories, moving them from short-term storage into long-term holding, **but new research** shows that it's not automatic. A night of z's is helpful **only if** you know a test is coming or, more generally, if you explicitly tell yourself you'll need the information in the future. In other words, don't expect eight hours of shut-eye to help you on a pop quiz.

In an elegant series of experiments, scientists at the University of Lübeck in Germany **tested** memory by having volunteers learn 40 word pairs, or the location of 15 cards in a Concentration-type game plus a sequence of finger taps (pinkie, index, forefinger…). Sleep **improved** retention only in those who **had been told** they'd be **tested** 10 hours later, not in those for whom the quiz **came** as a surprise, **says** a report in the *Journal of Neuroscience*. "Merely expecting that a memory will be used in a test determines whether sleep benefits its consolidation," **says** Lübeck's Jan Born.

(Sharon Begley , *Newsweek*, February 13, 2011)

[A] # Sleep Your Way to An "A"

Does this Title take you by surprise?

Why, or why not?

[B] Getting a good night's sleep has long been known to cement the day's memories, moving them from short-term storage into long-term holding, but new research shows that it's not automatic

What New information does this Lead Summary add to the Title? And what connector (linking expression) is used to signal the shift to the New?

has long been known: Do these words suggest that the facts known are

(a) well established and unquestionable?

(b) well established but questionable?

[C] Getting a good night's sleep **has long been known** to cement the day's memories, moving them from short-term storage into long-term holding, **but new research** shows that it's not automatic. A night of z's is helpful **only if** you know a test is coming or, more generally, if you explicitly tell yourself you'll need the information in the future. In other words, don't expect eight hours of shut-eye to help you on a pop quiz.

but: This connector usually introduces something which contrasts with previous information or a previous statement. What is the contrast here?

new research: Does the new research

(a) confirm what has long been known?

(b) show that there is something lacking or wrong in traditional knowledge?

only if: How does this ***if***-condition relate to the expression ***not automatic***?

In an elegant series of experiments: Is this phrase preparing us for

(a) the data of the new research?

(b) the conclusion of the new research?

[D] **In an elegant series of experiments**, scientists at the University of Lübeck in Germany **tested** memory by having volunteers learn 40 word pairs, or the location of 15 cards in a Concentration-type game plus a sequence of finger taps (pinkie, index, forefinger…). Sleep **improved** retention only in those who **had been told** they'd **be tested** 10 hours later, not in those for whom the quiz **came** as a surprise, **says** a report in the *Journal of Neuroscience*. "Merely expecting that a memory will be used in a test determines whether sleep benefits its consolidation," **says** Lübeck's Jan Born.

These are some of the verbs used in this paragraph:

tested   *improved*   *came*

These are all in the past tense. What justifies the use of the past tense?

(a) Arguing a point

(b) Reporting a series of events

(c) Giving a set of instructions

says…says: **Why is the present tense used here?**

(a) The report's and the scientist's statements are universally true.

(b) The two statements are part of the Conclusion.

DID YOU GET THAT?

Check the boxes below if you got the right answers.

[A] –Title

☐ ***Sleep Your Way to An "A"*** is a surprising title: normally you *work your way* to something desirable (e.g. success, the top).

[B] – Lead Summary

☐ The Lead Summary confirms the title's suggestion that sleep is desirable for work, stating that it has long been known to be good for memory. However, it introduces a further surprise: this benefit is *not automatic*. The shift to the New is signaled by the connector *but*.

☐ ***has long been known***: (a) well established and unquestionable.

[C], [D] – Body

☐ ***but***: We might think that a good night's sleep always cements memories: *but* introduces the counterclaim that this effect is *not automatic*.

☐ ***new research***: (b) Show that there is something lacking or wrong in traditional knowledge. *Research* usually aims to correct rather than confirm traditional knowledge. The use of the word *new* confirms that we are moving from Given to New.

☐ ***only if***: *Not automatic* implies that there was at least one condition. *Only if* reveals that there is in fact only one condition, before stating what that condition is.

☐ ***In an elegant series of experiments***: This phrase prepares us for (a) the data of the new research.

☐ *tested...improved...came*: (b) Reporting a series of past events. The past tense is generally used to report the process of collecting data.

☐ ***says...says***: (b) The present tense in these verbs accompanies a shift from reporting the data to indicating the researchers' conclusions.

☑ TASK 1

Complete the sentences below to produce a four-sentence version of the article in your own words.

Scientists have known for a long time that

Recently, however, some scientists have discovered that

The experiments they carried out basically

Their conclusion is that

 **GRAMMAR IN CONTEXT**

1. Verbs into nouns: -*ing* forms

Notice the words ending in *–ing* in the following sentence:

> **Getting** a good night's sleep has long been known to cement the day's memories, **moving** them from short-term storage into long-term **holding**, but new research shows that it's not automatic.

Similar forms, as shown in the first column below, appear in other places in the article. The meaning of each -*ing* form is given as a paraphrase and then the function is explained.

-*ing* Form	Paraphrase	Function
Getting a good night's sleep has long been known to cement the day's memories…	It has long been known that **if you get** a good night's sleep **this** cements the day's memories…	The *–ing* form here (sometimes called a *gerund*) makes the verb into a noun and simplifies the sentence structure: *Getting a good night's sleep* as grammatical subject – rather than the person getting the sleep – focuses attention on the process.
Merely **expecting** that a memory will be used in a test determines whether sleep benefits its consolidation…	**If you expect** that a memory will be used in a test, **this** determines whether sleep benefits its consolidation…	This gerund *–ing* form also functions as the grammatical subject of the sentence, again focusing attention on process rather than person.
scientists…tested memory by **having** volunteers learn 40 word pairs…	**The way** scientists tested memory **was to have** volunteers learn 40 word pairs…	The gerund *–ing* form here functions as the object of the preposition *by*. This use of the gerund saves space.
…**to cement the day's memories, moving** them from short-term storage into long-term…	…**to cement the day's memories, as it moves** them from short-term storage into long-term…	The *–ing* form here (sometimes called a *participle*) elaborates or expands on what precedes.
…from short-term storage into long-term **holding**…	…from short-term storage into long-term **place (in memory) where things are held**…	The *–ing* form here is part of a free-standing noun which happens to end in *–ing* – like *free parking, court hearing, happy ending.*

☑ TASK 2

The items in bold below can be simplified and made to focus more on process. See if you can convert them into gerund constructions. We have done the first example for you.

1. **If I have revised well the night before a big exam, it** makes me confident.

Revising well the night before a big exam makes me confident.

2. Peter likes **it when his daughter plays the piano.**

3. Isaac Newton astonished the world. **The way he did this was to discover the laws of motion.**

4. **To live in a country where no one speaks your language** can be very lonely at times.

5. **If a person goes without sleep for more than ten days, this** can cause some routine brain functions to close down.

6. Certain types of host can benefit from **it when they have parasitic organisms inside their digestive systems.**

☑ TASK 3

For each sequence of two sentences describing two actions, convert one into a participle form and attach it to the other sentence using a comma. We have done the first example for you.

1. **Libraries have always dealt with the business world. They have bought books, journals, and other products.**

   Libraries have always dealt with the business world, buying books, journals, and other products.

2. **Library patrons, moreover, are increasingly regarded as consumers. This view of library patrons has transformed user services into customer service.**

3. **These "big-deal" bundles tie up a huge portion of a library's budget. They make it difficult to trim when necessary.**

4. **Libraries today are mistaking a part of their mission for the whole. They are treating one of their most basic, mechanical, and least distinctive tasks as their dominant service.**

5. **Some students, faculty, and staff members have found in the reductions an offensive breach of democratic ideals. They have campaigned for a more humanistic approach to institutional belt-tightening.**

2. Compounds: Noun + Noun

Think about the use of noun + noun compounds (in bold):

Compound	Paraphrase	Function of compound
having volunteers learn 40 **word pairs**	having volunteers learn 40 **pairs of words**	Makes the text: shorter – no prepositions are required
a sequence of **finger taps**	a sequence of taps **with a finger**	simpler – no plural s or possessive 's or s' is required on the first noun

Research writing (itself a compound!) often makes use of such compounds to condense information.

☑ **TASK 4**

Consider the following plural nouns, pair them up as compounds, and regularize them by having the first Noun of the compound lose its plural marker –s.

cars   travels   affairs   parks   students   teams
thefts   members   tires   sets   plans   identities

1. ⎯⎯ travel plans ⎯⎯

2. ⎯⎯⎯⎯⎯⎯⎯⎯

3. ⎯⎯⎯⎯⎯⎯⎯⎯

4. ⎯⎯⎯⎯⎯⎯⎯⎯

5. ⎯⎯⎯⎯⎯⎯⎯⎯

6. ⎯⎯⎯⎯⎯⎯⎯⎯

☑ TASK 5

Consider the following phrases and shorten them into two- or three-word Noun + Noun compounds.

1. tube used for testing   *test tube*

2. pressure of your blood

3. someone's heart failing

4. machine which accelerates particles

5. laboratory where cancer is researched

6. car which is run by cell which produces energy from hydrogen

TEXT ORGANIZATION

☑ TASK 6

Argumentation

Think about the contrast presented in the following short text, then label each sentence in terms of what it does (i.e. what its function is), using the following labels:

Claim

Counter-claim

Support

Conclusion

Key indicators of the function of each part of the text have been underlined.

	Function
It is generally assumed that a good night's sleep is always a sure way of performing well in exams.	-----------------------------
However, new research suggests that this is not always the case.	-----------------------------
Data examined showed that unless the 'sleeper' focuses on a particular task before he or she goes to sleep, a good night's sleep is of no benefit.	-----------------------------
It can therefore be concluded that to gain from a good night's sleep you need the mind engaged.	-----------------------------

☑ TASK 7

Do the same for the following jumbled version of the model text for this Unit:

	Function
In other words, don't expect eight hours of shut-eye to help you on a pop quiz.	-------------------------------
Getting a good night's sleep has long been known to cement the day's memories, moving them from short-term storage into long-term holding,	-------------------------------
but new research shows that it's not automatic.	-------------------------------
A night of z's is helpful only if you know a test is coming or, more generally, if you explicitly tell yourself you'll need the information in the future.	-------------------------------

Exposition

Think about the following short text. It's of a type which we will call *Exposition*. Label each sentence in terms of its function, using the labels listed below:

Factual Statement

Supporting Detail 1

Supporting Detail 2   **(optional)**

Supporting Detail 3   **(optional)**

Concluding Statement (optional)

Segment	**Function**
'In short, merely expecting that a memory will be used in a test determines whether sleep benefits its consolidation,' says Lübeck's Jan Born.	-------------------------------
In one of the experiments, sleep improved retention only in those who had been told they'd be tested 10 hours later, not in those for whom the quiz came as a surprise.	-------------------------------
In an elegant series of experiments, scientists at the University of Lübeck in Germany tested memory by having volunteers learn 40 word pairs, or the location of 15 cards in a Concentration-type game plus a sequence of finger taps (pinkie, index, forefinger).	-------------------------------

☑ **TASK 8**

The Exposition text below has been jumbled. Use your understanding of the function of each segment to work out the original order, and then indicate the function and order of the segments in the right-hand column below.

Segment	Function	Order
The implications of this would make it unethical to keep dolphins captive in zoos and amusement parks, where 300,000 whales, dolphins and porpoises die each year.	----------------------------------	--------
They have far bigger brains and are brighter than chimpanzees and their communications are similar to those of humans, so much so that it has been suggested that they be re-categorized as "non-human persons".	----------------------------------	--------
Scientists have declared that dolphins are the world's second most intelligent creatures after humans.	----------------------------------	--------

Awareness

☑ TASK 9

In each of the the Conclusions sections of different articles shown below, we have underlined a segment. In the right-hand column, specify what function the underlined segment belongs to.

Given

New

Punchline (concludes the article explicitly and dramatically)

We have done the first item for you.

Conclusion	Function
Africans brought to the Americas as slaves continued this tradition, which gave their owners one more excuse to affect to despise them. Yet, as Dr Engel points out, Rwandan mountain gorillas eat a type of clay rather similar to kaolinite—the main ingredient of many patent medicines sold over the counter in the West for digestive complaints. <u>Dirt can sometimes be good for you, and to be "as sick as a parrot" may, after all, be a state to be desired.</u>	Punchline
This is what speech management looks like in 2010. No one elected Facebook or YouTube, and neither one is bound by the First Amendment. Nonetheless, it is their decisions that dictate, effectively, who gets heard. What's the answer? There is no easy answer. Monopolies like Google, Facebook, and Hollywood have certain advantages: That's why they tend to come into existence. That means the American public needs to be aware of the dangers that private censors can pose to free speech. The American Constitution was written to control abuses of power, but it didn't account for the heavy concentration of private power that we see today. <u>And in the end, power is power, whether in private or public hands.</u>	

<u>Since the 70s, obesity among children ages 6 to 11 has tripled</u>. Isn't it time for food manufacturers to step up their level of social responsibility? Don't our children deserve the best start in life? That includes healthy foods that grow healthy bodies. Marketing sugar- and chemical-laden "foods" to children lacks integrity and accountability. Is it any wonder so many children are overweight or obese: display unhealthy foods while they watch TV and… surprise, that's what they want to eat. It's like taking candy from a baby, or, um, GIVING candy to a baby.

Although not all anger derives from unfairness, <u>we might want to look further into whether people have a fairness instinct</u>. It could help us understand why certain policies are embraced and others resisted, why self-righteous anger is sometimes so easily elicited, and whether that anger is itself fair.

In the historical debate between mind and matter, mind won and silenced the voice of the body; it interpreted the body in terms of mind and considered it a mute machine that only reason could discover. <u>It is time to recover that physical voice, to recast the Epicurean thinking that puts pleasure in the place of thought, that imagines bodily pleasure to be a kind of thinking</u>. Good health will then be understood as a consequence of good pleasure, and adult pleasure will be prized, not *forbidden*; *controlled*, not censored; *enjoyed*, not feared.

Different segments of the Conclusion to the article "Animal Doctors" carry out these functions as follows:

Segment	Function
Africans brought to the Americas as slaves continued this tradition, which gave their owners one more excuse to affect to despise them.	Given
Yet, as Dr Engel points out, Rwandan mountain gorillas eat a type of clay rather similar to kaolinite—the main ingredient of many patent medicines sold over the counter in the West for digestive complaints.	New
Dirt can sometimes be good for you, and to be "as sick as a parrot" may, after all, be a state to be desired.	Punchline

How To

Write a Body and a Conclusion

The Body

Make sure that the **Body** of your paper has the following elements:

- A presentation of the **Given**, problematic situation which you will deal with;

- A presentation of the **New** proposal which your paper will put forward as a solution to the problem.

In the presentation of the **Given** or the **New**, use **Exposition** or **Argumentation** as appropriate (Unit D and Unit E will deal with these formats extensively).

The Conclusion

Make sure that the **Conclusion** of your paper has

- A brief re-statement of the **Given**

- A brief re-statement of the **New**

- A **Punchline**, a finale, a dramatic close

ASSIGNMENT

Recall the Given and New topics you worked on in Units A and B:

Globalization

Social networking sites

TV violence

Unhappy childhood

Shopping malls

Write the Body and Conclusion of a short paper on one of the topics. First, present the case for the Given (e.g. "Globalization is a form of progress") in 4 sentences. Then present a New position (e.g. "Globalization is a form of decline"). Support your New position with appropriate evidence. Then write a short Conclusion.

The following is a tentative outline, with suggested wordings for the transitions.

It is generally assumed…

- Point 1
- Point 2
- Point 3

However…

- Point 1
- Point 2
- Point 3

To conclude…

- Re-state Given
- Re-state New
- Punchline

SUMMARIZING AND REPORTING

UNIT FOCUS

In this Unit, you will be able to see:

■ How writers refer to the work of others (by **quoting**, **paraphrasing**, or **summarizing**);

■ How we can **summarize** research in different ways:

- By a short, "In-text" Summary;
- By a longer, "Stand-alone" Summary.

CONTEXT

1. Think about the following claim in the form of a statement: "Cats are smarter than dogs." If you asked your friends and family about this claim, do you think they would

   (a) agree?

   (b) disagree?

2. Why do you think people might generally agree that "cats are smarter than dogs"?

3. If we were to carry out some good research on this issue, what do you think the research would show?

   (a) Cats are better than dogs at understanding cause-and-effect connections between objects.

   (b) Cats are worse than dogs at understanding cause-and-effect connections between objects.

   (c) Cats are about the same as dogs in understanding cause-and-effect connections between objects.

4. For the sake of argument, let's assume that research found (b) to be the case. What kind of data (evidence, examples) do you think would support (b)?

(a) Comparing how long on average it takes dogs and cats to catch mice and rats.

(b) Comparing the ratio of brain mass to overall body mass in cats and dogs.

(c) Comparing the success of cats and dogs at performing in a practical task where success depends on recognizing a physical connection between two different objects.

5. Assuming that (c) is the correct answer and cats do indeed perform worse on the test than dogs do, what do you think would be the most plausible Conclusion for the research?

(a) Cats are not as clever as their owners often think they are.

(b) Cats' success at hunting must depend on supernatural rather than natural abilities.

(c) Cats and dogs think similarly but cats are clumsier than dogs.

WORDS IN CONTEXT

Using a dictionary if necessary, make sure you understand each word in bold and check the box before moving to the next item.

an **outsmarted** chess-player has been *defeated by a better player*	☐
feline (*related to cats*) intelligence	☐
a **baited** mousetrap has cheese on it *to attract mice*	☐
to **fathom** (*understand*) something which was previously a mystery	☐
Disney movies are **anthropomorphic** when they *make animals appear like humans*	☐

THE TEXT

Now you are ready to read the text.

a. First, skim through the whole text to get the general idea (or gist) of what the text is about.

b. Then read the text as broken down into sections, answering the questions. (Some multiple-choice items may have more than one correct answer.)

Cats outsmarted in psychologist's test

Strings experiment shows limits of feline intelligence.

It will cause **outrage** among some cat owners, **but** research suggests that pets are not as clever as some humans assumed – or at least that they think in a way we have yet to fathom.

Psychology lecturer Britta Osthaus says cats do not understand cause-and-effect connections between objects. She **tested** the thought processes of 15 of them by attaching fish and biscuit treats to one end of a piece of *string*, placing them under a plastic screen to make them unreachable and then seeing if the cats could work out that pulling on the other end of the string would pull the treat closer.

They were tested in three ways, using a single baited string, two parallel strings where only one was baited, and two crossed strings where only one was baited.

The single string test proved no problem, but unlike dogs (which Osthaus had previously tested) no cat consistently chose correctly between two parallel strings. With two crossed strings, one cat always made the wrong choice and others succeeded no more than might be expected by **chance**.

Osthaus, of Canterbury Christ Church University, Kent, said: "This finding is somehow surprising as cats regularly use their paws and claws to pull things towards them during play and hunting. They performed even worse than dogs, which can at least solve the parallel string task."

The study helped show the limits of feline intelligence, said Osthaus, who conducted the research while a teaching fellow at Exeter University. "If we know their limits we won't expect too much of them, which in turn is important for their welfare. I am not trying to say cats are stupid, just they are different. We are so anthropomorphic we can't see the world through their eyes."

There is just one consolation. Humans don't understand string theory either.

(James Meikle, *The Guardian*, June 16, 2009)

Cats outsmarted in psychologist's test

Cats outsmarted **means that**
(a) cats were smarter than other animals.
(b) other animals were smarter than cats.

As a title, *Cats outsmarted in psychologist's test* is a shortened form for what?
(a) Cats outsmarted other animals in a psychologist's test.
(b) Cats were outsmarted by other animals in a psychologist's test.

Strings experiment shows limits of feline intelligence

limits**: Does this word indicate that cats are**
(a) very smart, as has always been thought?
(b) not as smart as it has always been thought?

What makes this Lead Summary effective and attention-grabbing?

[A] It will cause **outrage** among some cat owners, **but** research suggests that pets are not as clever as some humans assumed – or at least that they think in a way we have yet to fathom.

In this Overview, why would this new research *outrage* cat owners? Is it because
(a) cat owners always think that their cats are smart?
(b) cat owners always think that their cats are not smart at all?

If the correct answer is (a) above, what will the connector *but* introduce?
(a) Evidence that cats are smart.
(b) Evidence that cats are not smart, after all.

Does the sentence following the *but* contain
(a) only the Given?
(b) only the New?
(c) both the Given and the New?

If (c) is correct, put a circle round the Given signal, and underline what signals the New.

[B] **Psychology lecturer Britta Osthaus says** cats do not understand cause-and-effect connections between objects. She **tested** the thought processes of 15 of them by attaching fish and biscuit treats to one end of a piece of *string*, placing them under a plastic screen to make them unreachable and then seeing if the cats could work out that pulling on the other end of the string would pull the treat closer.

The name of the researcher and the fact that she *says*, *tested*, etc., indicate that this is

(a) a report of what the researcher did.

(b) an argument against what the researcher did.

Does this report of the *string* experiment count as Conclusion or Data?

[C] They were tested in three ways, using a single baited string, two parallel strings where only one was baited, and two crossed strings where only one was baited.

The single string test proved no problem, but unlike dogs (which Osthaus had previously tested) no cat consistently chose correctly between two parallel strings. With two crossed strings, one cat always made the wrong choice and others succeeded no more than might be expected by **chance**.

***chance*. Does this say positive things about the cats' performance or does it report poor performance by cats?**

[D] Osthaus, of Canterbury Christ Church University, Kent, said: "This finding is somehow surprising as cats regularly use their paws and claws to pull things towards them during play and hunting. They performed even worse than dogs, which can at least solve the parallel string task."

What justifies the use of a quotation?

(a) Only the vividness and expressiveness of the speaker.

(b) Only the authority and credibility of the speaker.

(c) Both the vividness and authority of the speaker.

Support your answer with evidence from the text.

Do you detect a subtle reference to the Given assumption that cats are

(a) generally thought to be smart?

(b) generally thought to be stupid?

[E] **The study helped show the limits of feline** intelligence, said Osthaus, who conducted the research while a teaching fellow at Exeter University. "If we know their limits we won't expect too much of them, which in turn is important for their welfare. I am not trying to say cats are stupid, just they are different. We are so anthropomorphic we can't see the world through their eyes."

There is just one consolation. Humans don't understand string theory either.

In this Conclusion paragraph, can you identify reference to the Given and New, that cats are generally thought to be smart but in actual fact they are not?

What justifies the use of a quotation?
(a) Only the vividness and expressiveness of the speaker.
(b) Only the authority and credibility of the speaker.
(c) Both the vividness and the authority of the speaker.

Support your answer with evidence from the text.

Would you say this punchline relies on
(a) sarcasm?
(b) humor?

DID YOU GET THAT?

Check the boxes below if you got the right answers.

Title

☐ *Cats outsmarted*: (b) other animals were smarter than cats.

☐ **title**: (b) Cats were outsmarted by other animals in a psychologist's test.

Lead Summary

☐ *limits*: (b) This word indicates less intelligence than previously thought. A creature of limited intelligence is not outstandingly intelligent.

☐ **Why is it effective?** It summarizes Given and New.

☐ **Why is it attention-grabbing?** It makes us curious about the string experiment. Cats are known for playing with string – the idea of an experiment with it is intriguing.

[A] – Overview

☐ *outrage*: (a) cat owners always think that their cats are smart. Again, the writer anticipates a negative reaction from proud cat owners. This is a stereotype which is used in the Conclusion again for humorous effect. *Outrage* is a very strong word, an exaggeration for comic effect.

☐ *but*: (b) evidence that cats are not smart after all. The word implies a contrast between what cat owners stereotypically believe and what the "research suggests."

☐ (c) both the Given and the New.

☐ **Given:** *some humans assumed*

☐ **New:** *research suggests*

[B], [C], [D] – Body

☐ **The name of the researcher and the fact that she *says*, *tested*, etc.**: (a) a report of what the researcher did.

☐ *string* **experiment**: Experiments generally form part of Data. We already know from the Title and Lead Summary that the results of the research, and therefore what is put in the Conclusion, relate to cats' intelligence in general, not their performance on particular tasks.

☐ *chance*: Poor performance: if cats were smart, we would expect them to succeed more often than would be predicted by chance.

☐ **Justification for quotation** (*"This finding…"*):

(c) Both the vividness and the authority of the speaker.

- ☐ **Vividness**: The researcher uses everyday rather than scientific language: *somehow surprising, even worse than dogs* and *can at least.*

- ☐ **Authority**: The researcher is a credible witness concerning her own research. The name of her university adds institutional authority to her personal authority.

- ☐ **subtle reference to Given**: (a) *even worse than dogs* and *at least* both address the Given that *cats are generally thought to be smart*, by showing that cats are not only less smart than humans but less smart than dogs.

[E] – Conclusion

- ☐ **Reference to Given**: *we won't expect too much of them.*

- ☐ **Reference to New**: *the limits of feline intelligence.*

- ☐ **Justification for quotation ("*If we know their limits…*")**: This quotation is again (c) both vivid and authoritative.

  - ☐ **Vividness**: e.g. *we can't see the world through their eyes.*

  - ☐ **Authority**: Again, the speaker has natural authority as the person who did the research.

- ☐ **punchline**: (a) humor: The article returns to the comic theme of consoling cat owners who may be disappointed at the New. It also adds a pun (or play on words): *string theory* is a branch of theoretical physics, famous for being understandable only by Einstein-like geniuses.

☑ TASK 1

Complete the sentences below to produce a four-sentence summary of the article without repeating the exact wordings of the original.

Scientists have known for a long time that

Recently, however, some scientists have discovered that

The experiments they carried out basically

Their conclusion is that

 # GRAMMAR IN CONTEXT

1. The Passive

Note the use of the passive in the examples in the first column below:

Passive	Paraphrase (Active)	Function of Passive
Cats [were] **outsmarted** in [a] psychologist's test	**Something or someone outsmarted** cats in a psychologist's test	The passive either avoids or delays mentioning the agent, the person or thing responsible for the process described in the verb. This focuses attention on the process.
They **were tested** in three ways…	**Something or someone tested** cats in three ways…	
…two parallel strings where only one **was baited**, and two crossed strings where only one **was baited**.	…two parallel strings… and two crossed strings where **someone had** only **baited** one string.	
…no more than might be expected by **chance**.	…no more than **someone might expect** by chance	

Using the the passive is very common in research reporting because it helps focus readers' attention away from the individuals who carry out the research and onto the processes being researched.

☑ TASK 2

Convert the active verbs in the following sentences into passives. Decide whether or not it is important to identify the agent (the subject in these active sentences) and either include the agent in a *by*-phrase after the verb or delete the agent, as you consider most appropriate. We have done the first example for you.

1. **Thieves stole my laptop yesterday.**

My laptop was stolen yesterday.

(exclude *by thieves* as obvious and unnecessary)

2. **Aluminum may cause Alzheimer's Disease.**

3. **They grow a lot of rice in the USA.**

4. **Someone assassinated Martin Luther King in 1968.**

5. **Marine biologists are investigating the intelligence of dolphins.**

6. **Researchers have heated the new compound to 800 degrees Celsius.**

7. **A Belgian astronomer, Georges Lemaître, first proposed the Big Bang theory.**

2. Reporting tenses: Present and Past

Note especially the difference between the tenses (past and present) used to report information in the extracts below.

Present	Past	Meaning of tense
…research **suggests** that… Psychology lecturer Britta Osthaus **says**…		The present tense is used here to emphasize that the information being reported is considered to be new or current.
…pets **are** not as clever as some humans assumed… …cats **do not understand** cause-and-effect connections between objects. …they **are** different… Humans **don't understand** string theory either.		The present tense is used here to convey that the information being reported is general or universal ("timeless").
	She **tested** the thought processes of 15 of them They **were tested** in three ways	The past tense is used here to report a narrative sequence of events (the steps in the experiment).
	Osthaus, of Canterbury Christ Church University, Kent, **said**: "This finding… The study **helped** show the limits of feline intelligence, **said** Osthaus	The past tense is used here to indicate a narrative sequence (a report of what the researcher said).

☑ TASK 3

In the following report, use the notes above to help you choose the most appropriate tense, past or present, for the verbs in bold. We have done the first one for you.

Cancer survivors [**are** / **were**] no more likely to stop smoking, cut down on alcohol, or exercise more often than the general population, [**says** / **said**] new research published in the *British Journal of Cancer* today.

By comparing cancer survivors with others, the researchers [**find** / **found**] that the cancer survivors [**are** / **were**] less active overall and led a more sedentary lifestyle. Alcohol consumption and smoking [**decreases** / **decreased**] over time in both groups – but a cancer diagnosis [**does** / **did**] not give any extra motivation.

Speaking at a cancer research conference, researcher Jane Wardle [**says,** / **said,**] "You would expect a cancer diagnosis to act as a 'wake-up call', but in fact according to our study and several others most cancer patients [**do** / **did**] not change their unhealthy lifestyle choices."

TEXT ORGANIZATION

A. Quoting, Paraphrasing, Summarizing

To focus attention on the differences between *quoting*, *paraphrasing*, and *summarizing*, consider the following points and select what you think is the correct answer.

1. **When *citing* the work of others, we tend to quote word-for-word if the material is**
    (a) Of high literary value.
    (b) Written in a highly formal style.
    (c) Particularly striking in both form and content (i.e. both vivid and authoritative).

2. **What do we do if the material we want to cite is highly authoritative but not particularly vivid?**
    (a) We quote it.
    (b) We paraphrase or summarize it.

3. **What if the material we want to cite is neither authoritative nor vivid?**

    (a) We quote it.

    (b) We paraphrase or summarize it.

4. **Summaries present facts. What do we do if, in addition to facts, we have *opinions* to convey?**

    (a) We produce a longer summary.

    (b) We make it clear to the reader that we are no longer summarizing another source and are making an argument of our own.

B. More on Exposition

We indicated in the previous Unit (Unit C) that exposition involves at least two elements which are essential, or obligatory:

Factual Statement
Supporting Detail 1

Check back in Unit C if you can't recall.

☑ TASK 4

The following sentences all provide Supporting Details for Factual Statements. For each Supporting Detail, try to provide an appropriate associated Factual Statement. The Factual Statement should be a general claim or principle which the Detail can be used to support.

We have done the first example for you.

1. Dolphins have far bigger brains than chimpanzees and their communications are similar to those of humans. [Supporting Detail]

Scientists have declared that dolphins are the world's second most intelligent creatures after humans. [Factual Statement]

2. YouTube, for instance, has to constantly decide what to censor.

3. In 2006, Americans spent about $35 billion on diets and diet services, in large part under the illusion that they were improving their health.

4. The "big five" – Hinduism, Buddhism, Judaism, Christianity, and Islam – still dominate, but they are just the beginning.

5. One especially disturbing example of primate vivisection is a decades-long series of experiments performed on rhesus monkeys to learn more about the neuronal circuitry of the brain.

☑ TASK 5

In the following sentences we provide actual Factual Statements for each of the Supporting Details in the previous Task. Try to match each Factual Statement with its Supporting Detail.

[A] The luckless monkeys undergo multiple surgeries to have coils implanted in both eyes; holes drilled in their skulls to allow researchers to selectively destroy some parts of their brains and put recording electrodes in others; and head-immobilization surgeries in which screws, bolts, and plates are directly attached to their skulls.

[5   ]

[B] If you looked at the religious preferences that incoming students checked off as they entered college this fall, you might think that college campuses are diverse. They are. In fact, they are more diverse than you think.

[   ]

[C] Scientists have declared that dolphins are the world's second most intelligent creatures after humans.

[   ]

[D] On a daily basis, as we speak, Internet companies are making speech-related decisions more important than those made by any government.

[   ]

[E] In the United States, health has become a commodity and an industry.

[   ]

C. Expository Summaries

The Summary is a common way of providing an Exposition.

Note how, in a Summary, the first sentence contains

- A thesis statement, e.g. cats do not understand cause-and-effect connections;

- An attribution of the statement to a specified source, e.g. *Psychology lecturer Britta Osthaus says*.

These are the *obligatory* elements in any summary. We can also add a number of *optional* elements:

Thesis Statement + Attribution (essential)
Supporting Detail 1 (optional)
Supporting Detail 2 (optional)
Supporting Detail 3 (optional)
Concluding Statement (optional)

The following is an authentic example illustrating the above scheme of optional elements:

Segment	Function
Psychology lecturer Britta Osthaus says cats do not understand cause-and-effect connections between objects.	Attribution + Thesis Statement
She tested the thought processes of 15 of them by attaching fish and biscuit treats to one end of a piece of string,…	Supporting Detail 1
They were tested in three ways,…	Supporting Detail 2
The single string test proved no problem, but unlike dogs (which Osthaus had previously tested) no cat consistently chose correctly between two parallel strings.	Supporting Detail 3

Osthaus, of Canterbury Christ Church University, Kent, said: "This finding is somehow surprising as cats regularly use their paws and claws to pull things towards them during play and hunting...." | Concluding Statement

A Summary incorporated within a sentence or a paragraph is an "In-text" Summary. Summaries can vary enormously in length. At one end of the scale, a Summary can consist of a single sentence containing the elements of Thesis Statement and Attribution. At the other end of the scale, a Summary may be very long, containing many paragraphs with Supporting Details (optional) and a Conclusion (optional), including what we will call a "Stand-alone" Summary.

Stand-alone Summary

Sometimes, students are required to write "Stand-alone" Summaries, of important readings, for example. In a Stand-alone Summary, it is normal to include at least one Supporting Detail and a Concluding Statement.

Note that in a Stand-alone Summary, once the initial Attribution (*X said*) has been made, you don't have to repeat the same Attribution for any of the subsequent elements. All elements will be automatically understood by the reader as coming from the source (i.e. the writer or the article) stated in the opening Attribution.

Awareness

☑ TASK 6

We set out below some examples of short summaries. See if you can identify the functional elements in each summary. We have done the first example for you. As we show in the example, for each thesis statement, underline the particular words which attribute it to a specific source.

Summary 1

Segment	**Element**
<u>Researchers from Britain and the United States</u> ... <u>found that</u> people who did less well at school had shorter telomeres, suggesting they may age faster.	Attribution (Underlined) + Thesis Statement
Telomeres are sections of DNA that cap the ends of chromosomes, protecting them from damage.	Supporting Detail 1
The study participants were separated into four education groups...	Supporting Detail 2

Summary 2

> Sleep improved retention only in those who had been told they'd be tested 10 hours later, not in those for whom the quiz came as a surprise, says a report in the Journal of Neuroscience.
>
> "Merely expecting that a memory will be used in a test determines whether sleep benefits its consolidation," says Lübeck's Jan Born.

Concluding Statement

Summary 3

> In 2009, Killingsworth and Harvard psychologist Daniel Gilbert…launched a study on a Web site called Track Your Happiness.org.
>
> After answering basic questions about their age, location…, iPhone owners could sign up to receive one or more text messages a day.
>
> These texts nudged them to visit an online survey…
>
> Subjects also recorded whether…

Supporting Detail 3

Summary 4

> Michael Huffman and Mohamedi Seifu…noticed that local chimpanzees suffering from intestinal worms would dose themselves with the pith of a plant called veronia.
>
> This plant produces poisonous chemicals called terpenes….

How To

Write a Summary

Obligatory elements

Make sure that any **Summary** you write, whether **"in-text"** or **"stand-alone,"** has the following elements:

- A **Thesis Statement**
- An **Attribution** of the Thesis Statement to a specified source

Optional elements

- In addition to the above obligatory elements, the context sometimes requires us to add one or more optional elements (i.e. **Supporting Detail 1**, **Supporting Detail 2**, etc.).

ASSIGNMENT

Using the Internet, find two articles on the causes of obesity. Write a summary of each one (300–350 words) which contains all of the elements listed below:

Thesis Statement + Attribution

Supporting Detail 1

Supporting Detail 2

Supporting Detail 3

Other Supporting Details, as appropriate

Concluding Statement

THE EXPLANATORY SYNTHESIS

UNIT FOCUS

In this Unit, you will be able to see:

- How writers string together several Summaries to form an **Explanatory Synthesis**;

- What an Explanatory Synthesis looks like viewed "from above" as a macro-structure;

- What your role as a writer is in forming an Explanatory Synthesis.

CONTEXT

1. Think about the following statement: "The main cause of increasing childhood obesity is inactivity while watching TV." If you asked your friends and family about this claim, do you think they would

   (a) agree?

   (b) disagree?

2. Why could there be general agreement with the statement?

3. If we were to carry out some research on this issue, what do you think it would show?

   (a) Because children today watch more TV than in the past, they are less active and thus more likely to become obese.

   (b) Because TV advertising of unhealthy foods occurs most often at times when children are watching, TV advertising not TV watching is the main cause for growing childhood obesity.

4. For the sake of argument, let's assume that research found (b) to be true. What kind of data (evidence, examples) would we need to prove (b)?

   (a) Comparing obesity statistics in two groups of children: (i) those watching TV several hours a day and (ii) those not watching TV at all.

(b) Comparing the amount of unhealthy food advertising: (i) during times when children are likely to be watching and (ii) during times when children are unlikely to be watching.

5. Let's assume that researchers have indeed found that TV advertising of unhealthy foods during children's programs is the main cause of increasing obesity among children. Which of the following do you think is the most plausible conclusion we can draw?

(a) Governments should regulate advertising of unhealthy foods during children's programs.

(b) Parents should stop their children watching TV.

WORDS IN CONTEXT

Using a dictionary if necessary, make sure you understand each word in bold and check the box before moving to the next item.

An **impressive** (*remarkable*) new study	☐
new study was **released** (*published*)	☐
researchers **reviewed** (*examined; evaluated*)	☐
came to similar conclusions (*reached almost the same result*)	☐
unhealthy food (*like candy*)	☐
sugar- and chemical-**laden** (*full of; filled with*) "foods"	☐
obesity (*being overweight*)	☐
Is it any wonder (*It is not surprising that*) so many children are overweight or obese?	☐
getting children to (*persuading them to*)	☐
children's **exposure to** (*viewing of*) advertising	☐
television advertising **is to blame** (*is the cause of a negative effect*)	☐
reduce (*lessen*) their hours of television viewing	☐
deserve the best **start in life** (*a good beginning*)	☐
Isn't it time (*before it is too late*) for **food manufacturers** (*the food industry*) to **step up** (*increase; become more aware of*) their level of social responsibility	☐☐ ☐
integrity (*being true and honest*)	☐
accountability (*being responsible for what you do*)	☐

THE TEXT

Now you are ready to read the text.

a. First, skim through the whole text to get the general idea (or gist) of what the text is about.

b. Then read the text as broken down into sections, answering the questions. (Some multiple-choice items may have more than one correct answer.)

TV Ads Linked to Childhood Obesity

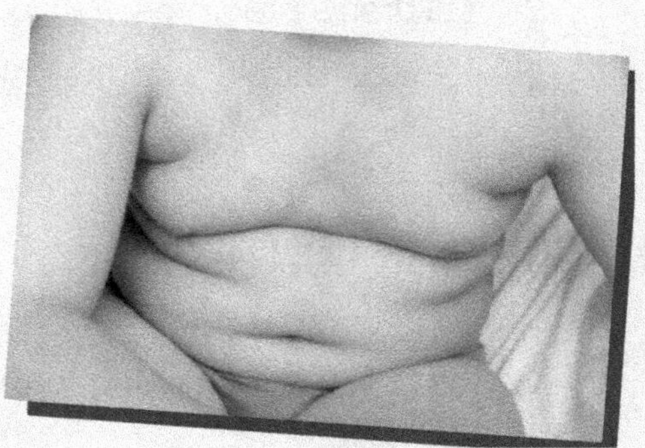

An impressive new study was released in the *American Journal of Public Health* linking television viewing to childhood obesity. Australian researchers found that the number of unhealthy foods advertised were highest during the hours children were most likely to be watching TV.

An impressive new study was released in the *American Journal of Public Health* linking television viewing to childhood obesity. Australian researchers reviewed television food advertising throughout Australia, Asia, Western Europe, and North and South America, **to determine** the dietary significance of children's exposure to advertising of unhealthy food items. In all countries examined, **the researchers found** that the number of unhealthy foods advertised were highest during the hours children were most likely to be watching TV.

While it may seem likely that hours in front of the television are hours that kids could be more active, research by scientists at The University of California, Los Angeles came to **similar** conclusions as the Australian scientists: television advertising is to blame. **The scientists found** that the number of advertisements for unhealthy foods was highest during the hours children watch TV—in all countries tested. The scientists concluded that getting children to reduce their hours of television viewing was an important factor in reducing childhood obesity.

Since the 70s, obesity among children ages 6 to 11 has tripled. Isn't it time for food manufacturers to step up their level of social responsibility? Don't our children deserve the best start in life? That includes healthy foods that grow healthy bodies. Marketing sugar- and chemical-laden "foods" to children lacks integrity and accountability. Is it any wonder so many children are overweight or obese: display unhealthy foods while they watch TV and…surprise, that's what they want to eat. It's like taking candy from a baby, or, um, **GIVING** candy to a baby.

(Michelle Schoffro Cook, http://www.care2.com/greenliving/tv-ads-linked-to-childhood-obesity.html, March 3, 2011)

TV Ads Linked to Childhood Obesity

An impressive new study was released in the *American Journal of Public Health* linking television viewing to childhood obesity. Australian researchers found that the number of unhealthy foods advertised were highest during the hours children were most likely to be watching TV.

Is this title surprising or unsurprising? Why?
Can you attempt a catchier, more attention-grabbing title?

The journal which publishes this article normally uses the initial two or three sentences of the article (the Overview) as Lead Summary. Why do you think this strategy works on this occasion?
(a) These sentences contain only the Given questionable assumption.
(b) These sentences contain only the New proposal.
(c) These sentences contain the Given and the New, which are both essential in a Lead Summary.

Can you paraphrase the two sentences using language that is more attention-getting and therefore more appropriate for a Lead Summary?

[A] An impressive new study was released in the *American Journal of Public Health* linking television viewing to childhood obesity. Australian researchers reviewed television food advertising throughout Australia, Asia, Western Europe, and North and South America, **to determine** the dietary significance of children's exposure to advertising of unhealthy food items. In all countries examined, **the researchers found** that the number of unhealthy foods advertised were highest during the hours children were most likely to be watching TV.

What job does the underlined initial sentence do in this Overview?
(a) It sets the scene.
(b) It provides details of a scene set.

How does the infinitive *to determine* support the initial sentence?
(a) By stating the aim of the New research.
(b) By documenting the Conclusion of the New research.

***the researchers found*: Is this the**
(a) Given?
(b) New?
(c) Data?
(d) Conclusion?

[B] While it may seem likely that hours in front of the television are hours that kids could be more active, research by scientists at The University of California, Los Angeles came to **similar** conclusions as the Australian scientists: television advertising is to blame. **The scientists found** that the number of advertisements for unhealthy foods was highest during the hours children watch TV—in all countries tested. The scientists concluded that getting children to reduce their hours of television viewing was an important factor in reducing childhood obesity.

The Given in this Overview is implied. Can you make the Given more explicit?

***similar* is extremely important here in the sentence underlined, because**

(a) It links the two studies reported to each other.

(b) It indicates that the second study is less important than the first.

***The scientists found…* signals the**

(a) Given

(b) New

(c) Data

(d) Conclusion

Paragraphs A and B above have a remarkably similar structure, which goes something like this:

Thesis Statement

Concluding Statement

Can you fill in what should go in the blank?

[C] Since the 70s, obesity among children ages 6 to 11 has tripled. Isn't it time for food manufacturers to step up their level of social responsibility? Don't our children deserve the best start in life? That includes healthy foods that grow healthy bodies. Marketing sugar- and chemical-laden "foods" to children lacks integrity and accountability. Is it any wonder so many children are overweight or obese: display unhealthy foods while they watch TV and…surprise, that's what they want to eat. It's like taking candy from a baby, or, um, **GIVING** candy to a baby.

What is the purpose of these questions?
Isn't it…?
Don't…?
Is it…?
(a) To ask for information.
(b) To state a Given problem.
(c) To hint at a Given problem and at the same time suggest a New direction.

In the context of the whole article, is the last paragraph
(a) Simply adding entertainment for the reader?
(b) Stating a conclusion and calling for action?

***GIVING*: Why is this word capitalized?**

DID YOU GET THAT?

Check the boxes below if you got the right answers.

Title

☐ At first glance, the title *TV Ads Linked to Childhood Obesity* isn't surprising, as people commonly assume that TV watching leads to obesity. The word *ads* is possibly surprising, though, as we might assume that it is the watching of TV itself rather than what people actually watch which leads to obesity.

Lead Summary

☐ (c) These sentences contain the Given and the New, which are both essential in a Lead Summary.

[A] – Overview

☐ **What job...?**: (a) It sets the scene.

☐ *to determine*: (a) By stating the aim of the New research.

☐ *the researchers found*: (d) Conclusion.

[B] – Body

☐ **Given**: Inactivity makes children obese.

☐ *similar*: (a) It links the two studies reported to each other.

☐ *The scientists found...*: (d) Conclusion: this sentence is a detail supporting the initial statement's report of the scientists' *conclusions*.

☐ **similar structure**: The structure is that of a Summary, as we described in the previous Unit:

Thesis Statement

Supporting Detail

Concluding Statement

[C] – Conclusion

☐ **What is the purpose...?**: *Isn't it...? Don't...? Is it...?* (c) To hint at a Given problem and at the same time suggest a New direction.

☐ **In the context**: (b) Stating a conclusion and calling for action – specifically for food manufacturers to step up their level of social responsibility.

☐ ***GIVING***: The idiomatic expression *like taking candy from a baby* is normally used to indicate an action that, like stealing from a baby, is easy but unethical. By changing the verb from *taking* to *giving* and putting it in bold capital letters, the writer emphasizes her opinion that persuading children to buy unhealthy food (such as candy) is also easy but unethical.

☑ TASK 1

Complete the sentences below to produce a five-sentence summary of the article.

Scientists have known for a long time that

Recently, however, some scientists have discovered that

One study they carried out basically

Another experiment

These findings lead one to the conclusion that

 **GRAMMAR IN CONTEXT**

1. Using the *to*-Infinitive

Notice the different kinds of structure in which the *to*-infinitive occurs in the examples below.

Example	Structure	Other examples
…what they <u>want</u> to eat…	<u>verb</u> + *to*-infinitive	Kevin <u>likes</u> **to read**. May <u>hates</u> **to walk**. They <u>love</u> **to dance**.
…children were most <u>likely</u> **to be** watching TV.	<u>adjective</u> + *to*-infinitive	Bill is <u>able</u> **to read**. Sue is <u>afraid</u> **to watch**. Ted is <u>desperate</u> **to leave**.
Isn't it <u>time</u> for food manufacturers **to step up** their level of social responsibility?	<u>noun</u> + *to*-infinitive	<u>time</u> **to go** <u>space</u> **to breathe** <u>room</u> **to make** mistakes
…<u>getting children</u> **to reduce** their hours of television viewing	<u>verb</u> + <u>noun</u> + *to*-infinitive	Mary <u>likes Bill</u> **to read**. Eric <u>got the printer</u> **to work**. Ahmad <u>asked her</u> **to come**.
<u>Australian researchers reviewed television food advertising</u>…**to determine** the dietary significance of children's exposure to advertising of unhealthy food items.	<u>clause</u> + *to*-infinitive OR *to*-infinitive + <u>clause</u>	<u>Sam went to Japan</u> **to study** karate. <u>He'd bought the eggplant</u> **to make** moussaka. **To make** an omelette <u>you must break eggs</u>.

Note that the structure in the last section of the table can appear at either the front or the end of the clause which it modifies:

Australian researchers reviewed television food advertising…**to determine** the dietary significance of children's exposure to advertising of unhealthy food items.

To determine the dietary significance of children's exposure to advertising of unhealthy food items, Australian researchers reviewed television food advertising.

Note also that the function of the last structure, expressing purpose, is sometimes emphasized by being expanded into the phrase *in order to* + infinitive, e.g.

Sam went to Japan, **in order to study** karate.

In order to become a fossil, several things must happen.

☑ TASK 2

Now try to supply a word of the correct kind (verb, noun, or adjective) to fill the gaps in the following sentences. We have done the first example for you.

1. It's ___impossible___ to please all of the people all of the time.

2. Although technically birds, penguins are _____________ to fly.

3. All of the stakeholders _____________ to meet soon and discuss this problem.

4. _____________ other people to pay attention is the most difficult part of public speaking.

5. It took my father a lot of _____________ to get the head gasket replaced.

6. Because her son is so immature, Mary is _____________ to let him go out with his friends.

7. Although he was determined, Livingstone lacked the _____________ to continue his quest for the source of the Nile.

☑ TASK 3

Try to supply an appropriate ending or beginning to the following sentences expressing *purpose*.

1. In order to avoid a lot of frustration when you are visiting a new city

    ____

2. ____

    you've got to be a friend.

3. ____

    the researchers double-checked their equipment.

4. Christopher Columbus sailed across the Atlantic Ocean

    ____

2. *This* and *that*: Referring to previous text

Notice from the examples below how the pronouns *this* and *that* may refer to simple items or much broader concepts raised in the previous text.

Example	What the pronoun refers to
Is it any wonder so many children are overweight or obese: display unhealthy foods while they watch TV and…surprise, **that**'s what they want to eat.	unhealthy foods
Don't our children deserve the best start in life? **That** includes healthy foods that grow healthy bodies.	the best start in life
But is daydreaming good for us? **That**'s a tough question to answer, says Killingsworth.	But is daydreaming good for us?
The results showed that people with lower educational achievements had shorter telomeres, indicating that they may age faster, and the study also offered strong evidence that **this** is not affected by people's social and economic status later in life…	people with lower educational achievements had shorter telomeres, indicating that they may age faster
He showed a cause-and-effect relationship for samples that were several hours apart from each other, Barrett notes, but **that** says little about "shifts in consciousness [that] occur on the order of milliseconds."	He showed a cause-and-effect relationship for samples that were several hours apart from each other

Note also that *this* or *that* may refer to a whole paragraph, for example:

> Advertising experts know that if you repeat a message often enough, people will believe it, regardless of whether it's truthful or not. Repetition, we're told, is much more important than accuracy.
>
> Given **that**, I could easily have started believing false accusations about me.

☑ TASK 4

For each bold *this* or *that* pronoun in the following segments, underline the part of the text which you think the pronoun is referring to. We have done the first example for you.

1. The reason is simple: <u>Research universities use animals to do their research,</u> and we are OK with **that**.

2. Ah! I'm delighted to talk about the Duchess of Windsor. In fact, I happen to have her bracelet on right here. She gave **this** to me.

3. On April 12, 1961, Soviet cosmonaut Yuri Gagarin thrilled the world when he became the first human in space. In the Cold War politics of the time, **this** sent shock waves through the American people.

4. Reno Fire Chief Michael Hernandez says crews were able to stop the wall of flames before it reached Galena High School. **That**'s where Vice President Joe Biden spoke...

5. Whenever you search for someone or something, narrow down your criteria by selecting "People" or another category from the menu at the upper left of the search page. **This** will save you time...

6. ESPN2's viewers are up 12 percent to 299,000. **That**'s small compared to the numbers generated by Fox News.

TEXT ORGANIZATION

The Explanatory Synthesis as a style of writing

As we display in the text for this Unit, an Explanatory Synthesis is made up of more than one independent *Summary*. These Summaries could be about several different research studies, or about different aspects of the same study. Writers string together the various summaries in such a way as to provide an overall *Explanation*, *Narrative*, or *Description*.

If we look at the Explanatory Synthesis from above, it ideally has the following macro-structure:

Introduction

Summary 1

Summary 2

Summary 3

etc.

Overall Conclusion

What's your role as a writer in developing an Explanatory Synthesis?

To bring together (or *synthesize*) the various studies you have chosen to summarize you need to do the following tasks:

Introduction	set the scene by introducing the common topic which the various studies have researched into
Summary 1	use linking transitions to show the reader
Summary 2	• how the study relates to the topic
Summary 3	• similarities and differences between the studies you are summarizing
Overall Conclusion	generalize the findings of the studies and signal the end of synthesis

Words and phrases commonly used in transitions include the following types:

Exemplification	Addition	Contrast
for example	in addition	However
for instance	too	Nevertheless
	also	on the other hand
	similarly	
	moreover	
	furthermore	
such X	another X, a third X, a similar X, more X, other X	
in one X	other X	

Awareness

☑ TASK 5

The following pairs of segments form parts of larger Explanatory Syntheses. Underline the words in the second segment of each pair which link the two segments. We have done the first two examples for you.

Introduction – Summary 1

> A growing number of animal behaviourists now think that wild animals can and do deal with their own medical needs.

> William Karesh, of the Wildlife Conservation Society, in New York, <u>for example</u>, has studied the health of a wide range of wild animals, including anaconda snakes, macaws, …

Summary 1 – Summary 2

> An impressive new study was released in the *American Journal of Public Health* linking television viewing to childhood obesity. Australian researchers reviewed television food advertising…

> Research by scientists at The University of California, Los Angeles <u>came to similar conclusions as the Australian scientists</u>: television advertising …

Introduction – Summary 1

> It has also become clear that they are "cultural" animals, meaning that new types of behaviour can quickly be picked up by one dolphin from another.

> In one study, Diana Reiss, professor of psychology at Hunter College, City University of New York, showed that bottlenose dolphins could…

Summary 1 – Summary 2

> One example of self-medication was discovered in 1987. Michael Huffman and Mohamedi Seifu, working in the Mahale Mountains National Park in Tanzania, noticed that local chimpanzees suffering from intestinal worms would dose themselves with the pith of a plant called *veronia*…

> Since the *veronia*-eating chimps were discovered, more evidence has emerged suggesting that animals often eat things for medical rather than nutritional reasons…

☑ TASK 6

Now try to write a suitable first segment for the pairs below.

Summary 1 – Summary 2

Other observations also support the idea that clay is detoxifying… Elephants lick clay from mud holes all year round, … And the addition of clay to the diets of domestic cattle increases the amount of nutrients that they can absorb from their food by 10–20%.

Summary 1 – Summary 2

It turns out that <u>other animals exploit rough plants, too</u>… Canadian snow geese, just before they migrate, deposit huge quantities of undigested grass and tapeworms. Wolves eat grass to scour their guts of roundworms. And, according to Indian folklore, tigers, too, occasionally eat grass, probably for similar reasons.

☑ TASK 7

Now, try to write a suitable second segment for the pairs below, including some kind of linking transition.

Introduction – Summary 1

> Research has shown dolphins living in the wild co-operate in ways that imply complex social structures.

Summary 1 – Summary 2

> Last year a study published in *Nature* by Thomas Jacob of the University of Colorado, in Boulder, showed that glaciers in the Himalayas and Karakoram had lost little ice between 2003 and 2010, and that those on the Tibetan plateau itself were growing.

Explanatory Syntheses in Given and New

Note that an Explanatory Synthesis, like any individual Summary, may form part of either the Given or the New sections in your paper. In one paper, for example, you may wish to summarize both the several sources on which a Given position has traditionally been based and also the several more recent sources on which a New position is based.

How To

Write an Explanatory Synthesis

Make sure that your **Synthesis** has the following elements:

- An **Introduction**;
- **Summaries** of at least two different studies or two different aspects of one study;
- An **Overall Conclusion** (this is optional).

ASSIGNMENT

Using the Internet, try to find at least two popularized research articles on the subject of *daydreaming*. Summarize the articles and combine your Summaries into an Explanatory Synthesis (300–350 words) which contains all of the elements listed below:

Introduction

Summary 1

- Attribution + Thesis Statement
- Supporting Detail(s)
- Concluding Statement

Summary 2

- Attribution + Thesis Statement
- Supporting Detail(s)
- Concluding Statement

Summary X, etc.

- Overall Conclusion

Here are links to some articles you could use:

Daydreaming really is the key to solving complex problems
http://www.telegraph.co.uk/science/9695290/Daydreaming-really-is-the-key-to-solving-complex-problems.html

People spend 'half their waking hours daydreaming'
http://www.bbc.co.uk/news/health-11741350

The Power of Daydreaming
http://www.psychologytoday.com/blog/the-power-daydreaming/200906/whats-your-attitude-toward-daydreaming

Is Daydreaming Pathological?
http://www.psychologytoday.com/blog/beautiful-minds/201112/is-daydreaming-pathological

THE CRITIQUE AND THE PERSUASIVE SYNTHESIS

UNIT FOCUS

In this Unit, you will be able to see:

- How a **Counter-argument** functions as an element within a **Critique**;

- How several Critiques may be strung together to form a **Persuasive Synthesis**;

- What your role would be as an author in putting together a Critique and writing a Persuasive Synthesis.

CONTEXT

1. Think about the following statement: "Daydreaming makes you unhappy." What's your initial reaction to such a claim? Would you

   (a) Agree?

   (b) Disagree?

2. Why do you think people might generally agree that "Daydreaming makes you more content"?

3. If you were to carry out some research on this issue, what do you think the research would show?

   (a) Daydreaming makes you *happier* than you would otherwise be at the time you're doing it.

   (b) Daydreaming makes you *unhappier* than you would otherwise be at the time you're doing it.

4. For the sake of argument, let's assume that research found (b) to be the case. What kind of data (evidence, examples) would be needed to prove (b)?

   (a) Survey data on people's reports of their mood *at the time of* daydreaming.

   (b) Survey data on people's reports of their mood *after* daydreaming.

5. Assuming that (a) is the appropriate answer, what would be the most plausible Conclusion for the research?

   (a) Daydreaming has a negative effect on people's moods, whether it happens while doing something they enjoy or doing something they dislike.

   (b) Daydreaming has no effect on people's moods, whether it happens while doing something they enjoy or doing something they dislike.

WORDS IN CONTEXT

Using a dictionary if necessary, make sure you understand each word or phrase in bold and check the box before moving to the next item.

daydreaming (*fantasizing*), or **mind-wandering**	☐
distracted from the task (*not staying focused*)	☐
straying (*not staying focused*)	☐
mental drifting (*when your mind wanders or you think of something else*)	☐
nudged (*reminded*) them	☐
stimulus (*something that makes you act or react*)	☐
cause-and-effect relationships (*whether A causes B or A causes B*)	☐
gauge (*assess or evaluate*) the mental state of	☐
on the order of milliseconds (*in a fraction of a second*)	☐
hard to **scale up** (*difficult to do on a large scale*)	☐
downer (*a bad mood*)	☐
Snap out of it! (*Wake up from your daydream!*)	☐
stay cheerful (*be happy*)	☐
eloping (*running away to get married*)	☐
leaching away (*eroding; taking away bit by bit*)	☐
you're **better off** (*it would be preferable*)	☐

THE TEXT

Now you are ready to read the text.

a. First, skim through the whole text to get the general idea (or gist) of what the text is about.

b. Then read the text as broken down into sections, answering the questions. (Some multiple-choice items may have more than one correct answer.)

Daydreaming Is a Downer

Psychologists have found that people are distracted from the task at hand nearly half the time, and this daydreaming consistently makes them less happy

Snap out of it! That daydream you're having about eloping to the Bahamas with Johnny **Depp** or Angelina **Jolie** is leaching away your happiness. **In a new global study**, researchers used iPhones to gauge the mental state of more than 2000 volunteers several times a day—even when they were having sex. **The results indicate that**, if you want to stay cheerful, you're better off focusing on the present, no matter how unpleasant it is.

The human mind is remarkably good at straying from the moment. That ability allows us to remember the past, plan for the future, and "even imagine things that never occur at all," says Matthew Killingsworth, a doctoral student in psychology at Harvard University. "As a scientist, it's **something** I do all the time."

But is daydreaming good for us?

That's **a tough question to answer**, says Killingsworth. **To find out**, scientists must survey subjects several times a day to record their mood and activities at that exact moment. "People are quite good at telling you how happy they are right now," he says, "but less at telling you how happy they were last week." In the past, researchers have used buzzing pagers, which reminded volunteers to write in a diary, or they bought their subjects expensive mobile devices like Palm Pilots. Both methods are hard to scale up. So Killingsworth took advantage of something thousands of people already have and use all the time: iPhones.

In 2009, Killingsworth and Harvard psychologist Daniel Gilbert, with the help of a friend who is a software engineer, **launched a study** on a Web site called *Track Your Happiness.org.* iPhone owners could sign up to receive one or more text messages a day. These texts nudged them to visit an online survey to report how happy they were feeling and pick from 22 different choices, including shopping, watching television, or working, to describe what they were doing right then. Subjects also recorded whether they were thinking about that activity or about something else that was pleasant, neutral, or unpleasant.

When the researchers analyzed the experiences of a subset of 2250 adults, about three-quarters of them from the United States, the first thing they noticed was just how often people weren't thinking about what they were doing. Over all, subjects' minds were wandering about 47% of the time, the duo reports online today in *Science*. Only during sex did mind-wandering occur less than 30% of the time.

The daydreaming was not good for people's moods: Volunteers were unhappier when their thoughts were elsewhere. Statistical tests showed that mind-wandering earlier in the day correlated with a poorer mood later in the day, but not vice versa, suggesting that unhappiness with their current activity wasn't prompting people to mentally escape. Instead, their wandering minds were the cause of their gloom. Mental drifting was a downer for subjects during even the dullest activities, like cleaning, the researchers found.

The findings "challenge the foundations of psychology," says Lisa Feldman Barrett, a psychologist and neuroscientist at Northeastern University in Boston, who pioneered data gathering with Palm Pilots. Psychologists assume that the mind responds to a stimulus out in the world, but in this study, "it almost looks like the stimulus is irrelevant."

Still, says Barrett, the study has **limitations**. For one, not everyone can afford to own an iPhone, so the study sample may not be representative of the population. And as to whether mind-wandering was really the cause of subjects' unhappiness, Barrett would like to see stronger evidence. Killingsworth's statistical analysis "is a good start, but not a sufficient answer," she says. He showed a cause-and-effect relationship for samples that were several hours apart from each other, Barrett notes, but that says little about "shifts in consciousness [that] occur on the order of milliseconds."

(Lauren Schenkman, http://news.sciencemag.org/sciencenow/ 2010/11/ daydreaming-is-a-downer.html, November 11, 2010)

Daydreaming Is a Downer

This title takes us by surprise, because
(a) we assume daydreaming always makes us happy.
(b) we have always known daydreaming makes us sad.

Psychologists have found that people are distracted from the task at hand nearly half the time, and this daydreaming consistently makes them less happy

What does the Lead Summary add to the title?
(a) It restates a popular but erroneous assumption.
(b) It restates the surprising New finding.
(c) It restates the surprising New finding and adds other surprising information.

[1] Snap out of it! That daydream you're having about eloping to the Bahamas with Johnny **Depp** or Angelina **Jolie** is leaching away your happiness. **In a new global study**, researchers used iPhones to gauge the mental state of more than 2000 volunteers several times a day—even when they were having sex. **The results indicate that**, if you want to stay cheerful, you're better off focusing on the present, no matter how unpleasant it is.

Depp…Jolie: Why are movie stars mentioned here?

Does this paragraph focus on
(a) the Given misconception that daydreaming makes you happy?
(b) the New research that suggests daydreaming in fact makes you unhappy?

In a new global study: Is this
(a) a Given problem?
(b) part of the New insight?
(c) Data which support the New proposal?
(d) Conclusion?

The results indicate that: Is this part of the
(a) Given?
(b) New?
(c) Data?
(d) Conclusion?

[2] The human mind is remarkably good at straying from the moment. That ability allows us to remember the past, plan for the future, and "even imagine things that never occur at all," says Matthew Killingsworth, a doctoral student in psychology at Harvard University. "As a scientist, it's **something I do all the time**."

What is the something I do all the time?
(a) Daydreaming?
(b) Snapping out of daydreaming?

How is this referred to in the first paragraph?
(a) Snap out of it!
(b) That daydream you're having.

[3] But is daydreaming good for us?

How do you expect this question to be answered?
(a) "Yes, it is."
(b) "No, it is not."

What is the purpose of the question?
(a) To suggest something obviously true in an indirect way.
(b) To prepare the reader for upcoming discussion of research on daydreaming.

[4] That's a tough question to answer, says Killingsworth. **To find out**, scientists must survey subjects several times a day to record their mood and activities at that exact moment. "People are quite good at telling you how happy they are right now," he says, "but less at telling you how happy they were last week." In the past, researchers have used buzzing pagers, which reminded volunteers to write in a diary, or they bought their subjects expensive mobile devices like Palm Pilots. Both methods are hard to scale up. So Killingsworth took advantage of something thousands of people already have and use all the time: iPhones.

To find out signals that the paragraph will
(a) immediately answer the tough question.
(b) give supporting details of why the question is tough.

[5] In 2009, Killingsworth and Harvard psychologist Daniel Gilbert, with the help of a friend who is a software engineer, **launched a study** on a Web site called *Track Your Happiness.org*. iPhone owners could sign up to receive one or more text messages a day. These texts nudged them to visit an online survey to report how happy they were feeling and pick from 22 different choices, including shopping, watching television, or working, to describe what they were doing right then. Subjects also recorded whether they were thinking about that activity or about something else that was pleasant, neutral, or unpleasant.

launched a study: Is this paragraph about
(a) a new study?
(b) supporting details about the study already introduced?

What steps did the researchers follow in collecting the Data they finally opted for?

----

[6] **When the researchers analyzed** the experiences of a subset of 2250 adults, about three-quarters of them from the United States, the first thing they noticed was just how often people weren't thinking about what they were doing. Over all, subjects' minds were wandering about 47% of the time, the duo reports online today in *Science*. Only during sex did mind-wandering occur less than 30% of the time.

When the researchers analyzed: Is this paragraph about
(a) a new study?
(b) further supporting details about the study already introduced?

[7] **The daydreaming was not good** for people's moods: Volunteers were unhappier when their thoughts were elsewhere. Statistical tests showed that mind-wandering earlier in the day correlated with a poorer mood later in the day, but not vice versa, suggesting that unhappiness with their current activity wasn't prompting people to mentally escape. Instead, their wandering minds were the cause of their gloom. Mental drifting was a downer for subjects during even the dullest activities, like cleaning, the researchers found.

Does this paragraph show that
(a) people daydreamed because they were unhappy?
(b) people were unhappy because they daydreamed?

[8] **The findings "challenge** the foundations of psychology," says Lisa Feldman Barrett, a psychologist and neuroscientist at Northeastern University in Boston, who pioneered data gathering with Palm Pilots. Psychologists assume that the mind responds to a stimulus out in the world, but in this study, "it almost looks like the stimulus is irrelevant."

Is the discussion in this paragraph about
(a) Data?
(b) conclusions?
(c) limitations of the study?

[9] **Still**, says Barrett, the study has **limitations**. For one, not everyone can afford to own an iPhone, so the study sample may not be representative of the population. And as to whether mind-wandering was really the cause of subjects' unhappiness, Barrett would like to see stronger evidence. Killingsworth's statistical analysis "is a good start, but not a sufficient answer," she says. He showed a cause-and-effect relationship for samples that were several hours apart from each other, Barrett notes, but that says little about "shifts in consciousness [that] occur on the order of milliseconds."

Is *Still* a transition which indicates
(a) an addition?
(b) an example?
(c) a contrast?

Read on and list two limitations.

1.

2.

DID YOU GET THAT?

Check the boxes below if you got the right answers.

Title

☐ **Why surprising?** (a) we assume daydreaming makes us happy. Dreams, particularly daydreams, are usually thought of as pleasurable, indeed as strategies to escape pain. It therefore seems surprising, almost self-contradictory, to state that *Daydreaming is a downer.*

Lead Summary

☐ **What does it add?** (c) It restates the surprising New finding and adds other surprising information – *people are distracted from the task at hand nearly half the time.*

Paragraph [1]

☐ *Depp...Jolie*: Movie fans famously fantasize about glamorous movie stars in order to escape the ordinariness of their own lives. Whether or not such fantasizing makes one happy is the topic of the research described in this article.

☐ **Paragraph focus**: (b) the New research that suggests daydreaming in fact makes you unhappy.

☐ *In a new global study*: (c) Data which support the New proposal. The words *new* and *study* signal that scientists are again performing their role of changing our knowledge about the world.

☐ *The results indicate that*: (c) Data and (d) Conclusion. *The results* signal that what follows will summarize the Data and *indicate that* is a typical phrase to report Conclusions.

Paragraph [2]

☐ *something I do all the time*: **What is it?** (a) Daydreaming – imagining things that never occur at all, as Killingsworth expresses it.

☐ *something I do all the time*: **How is it referred to in the first paragraph?** (b) *That daydream you're having.*

Paragraph [3]

☐ **Answer expected?** (b) No, it is not.

☐ **Purpose of question?** (b) To prepare the reader for upcoming discussion of research on daydreaming.

Paragraph [4]

☐ *To find out*: (b) give supporting details of why the question is tough. If this were not the case, there would have been no mention of the question being *tough to answer.*

Paragraph [5]

- ☐ *launched a study*: (a) a new study. The word *launch* denotes a beginning of some kind.

- ☐ **Steps researchers followed in collecting Data**:

  1. Collected iPhone-owning volunteers as subjects via a website.

  2. Sent subjects phone messages at various times of day asking them to record

     (a) whether they were daydreaming or not.

     (b) whether the subject of their daydreams was pleasant, neutral, or unpleasant.

Paragraph [6]

- ☐ *When the researchers analyzed*: (b) further supporting details about the study already introduced. Use of the definite article for *the researchers* indicates we are hearing about researchers already known to us. *Analysis* is also a later stage of the research process.

Paragraph [7]

- ☐ *The daydreaming was not good*: (b) people were unhappy because they daydreamed. This paragraph compares the daydreaming data with the mood data to reach this conclusion, later restated as *their wandering minds were the cause of their gloom.* Note how this conclusion from research data reverses our likely New expectation that daydreaming will make us happier.

Paragraph [8]

- ☐ *The findings "challenge…"*: (b) conclusions. Rather than merely reporting the findings, this paragraph relates the findings of this experiment to the whole of psychology

Paragraph [9]

- ☐ *Still*: (c) a contrast: This connector introduces a counter-claim, a further discussion of the study which voices scientific concerns about whether the Data can really support the Conclusion enough for us to replace the Given with the New.

- ☐ **Limitations**:

  1. The people taking part in the experiment (*the study sample*), iPhone owners, *may not be representative of the population*.

  2. People's consciousness may shift very quickly (*on the order of milliseconds*), so we cannot be sure that the correlation of daydreaming earlier and poor mood later in the day is due to a *cause-and-effect relationship*.

☑ TASK 1

Complete the sentences below to produce a five-sentence summary of the article.

Scientists have known for a long time that

Recently, however, some scientists have discovered that

The experiment they carried out basically

These findings lead one to the conclusion that

However, another scientist argues that

 GRAMMAR IN CONTEXT

1. *If* and *when*: Real Conditional Clauses

Notice how *if* and *when* are used to introduce a subordinate clause which modifies the scope of the main clause. Such sentences are known as *conditional sentences*, and the *if*-clauses are known as *conditional clauses*.

Conditional Sentence	Function of Conditional Clause
...if you want to stay cheerful, you're better off focusing on the present, no matter how unpleasant it is. Volunteers were unhappier **when** their thoughts were elsewhere. **When** Cindy Engel notices that her cat, Darwin, has vomited on her carpet, she doesn't worry... A night of z's is helpful only **if** you know a test is coming...	Conditional clauses often describe a general truth or habit and imply a cause-and-effect relationship. These examples are of a type sometimes called "real conditionals" because they refer to real rather than imaginary situations.

Notice also that conditional clauses may appear *before* or *after* the main clause. If the conditional clause comes first, there is a pause, shown by a comma, between the clauses.

☑ TASK 2

Write a sentence containing a conditional clause for each of the situations below. We have done the first example for you.

1. **Some students have part-time jobs. The same students tend to get lower grades.**

   If students have part-time jobs, they tend to get lower grades.

   -

   -

2. **Some people educate themselves about the psychology of the opposite sex. These people have fewer marital problems.**

   -

   -

3. Earthquakes sometimes happen on islands. Such an event causes a tsunami.

----

4. Sometimes farmland gets overgrazed by livestock. In such cases, the soil erodes and the land becomes a desert.

----

5. The monsoon season occurs in Asia. A change in landmass temperature reverses wind direction.

----

6. Some creatures are better at adapting to temperature change than others. In a major climate change, such creatures survive.

----

2. Ellipsis: Leaving things out

Notice that some items seem to have been left out (or *ellipsed*) in the following sentence.

Ellipsed	Full
"People are quite good at telling you how happy they are right now," he says, "but less at telling you how happy they were last week."	"People are quite good at telling you how happy they are right now," he says, "but **they are** less **good** at telling you how happy they were last week."

Writers use *ellipsis* to eliminate repetition and help focus attention on ideas related to the words which remain.

☑ TASK 3

Indicate where words have been ellipsed from the following sentences and what these words would be. We have done the first example for you.

1. Killingsworth's statistical analysis "is a good start, but *it is*ⱽ not a sufficient answer," she says.

2. The problem ceases to exist in its original form and becomes more manageable and less threatening.

3. They performed surgery on the mice and did not provide post-operative analgesics.

4. "You don't have to be a stand-up comic to get your patients to relax, but just have a cheerful, spirited approach and be willing to respond to their humour."

5. By the end of the novel, Jane Bennet marries Mr. Bingley and Lizzie Bennet Mr. Darcy.

☑ TASK 4

See if you can use ellipsis to shorten the following sentences. Use brackets as shown to indicate the words to be ellipsed. We have done the first example for you.

1. Researchers sedated the animals, (they) administered the new drug, and (they) followed up with health checks every six months.

2. Bottle-nosed dolphins scored the highest and whales scored the lowest on a series of intelligence tests.

3. Students in the experimental group could perform better than others in exams, but they slept fewer hours than others.

4. Professionals planned meals, prepared meals, and cooked meals in their own home 27% less than unskilled laborers.

TEXT ORGANIZATION

1. More on Argumentation

Recall that Argumentation involves

Claim

Counter-claim

Support

Concluding Statement

Notice how the extract below from the text in this unit contains all these components.

Segment	Component	Function
The human mind is remarkably good at straying from the moment. That ability allows us to remember the past, plan for the future, and "even imagine things that never occur at all," says Matthew Killingsworth, a doctoral student in psychology at Harvard University. "As a scientist, it's something I do all the time."	Claim	states a Given
But is daydreaming good for us? That's a tough question to answer, says Killingsworth.	Counter-claim	brings out the New
To find out, scientists must survey subjects several times a day to record their mood and activities at that exact moment. When the researchers analyzed the experiences of a subset of 2250 adults…	Support	comes in the form of Data or other Supporting Details
Mental drifting was a downer for subjects during even the dullest activities, like cleaning, the researchers found.	Concluding Statement	wraps up the particular argument

2. The Critique

Argumentative writing commonly appears in a larger unit of writing, what we are calling the *Critique*. In a Critique the writer addresses a claim made by someone else (such as the claim made by a researcher who has carried out a study and has stated a New position). The Critique writer first *summarizes* and then *evaluates* the claim. The core of a critique is thus:

Summary of X

Evaluation of X

The Critique writer has two options for ordering the Summary material and the Evaluation material. We are calling these options **complete** and **point by point**:

Complete

Supporting Detail 1
Supporting Detail 2
Supporting Detail 3

Evaluation of Supporting Detail 1
Evaluation of Supporting Detail 2
Evaluation of Supporting Detail 3

Point by point

Supporting Detail 1

Evaluation of Supporting Detail 1

Supporting Detail 2

Evaluation of Supporting Detail 2

Supporting Detail 3

Evaluation of Supporting Detail 3

Note that Evaluation involves two possibilities for the Critique writer:

Positive: to **endorse** (or agree with) the claim and provide further supports;

Negative: to **rebut** (or argue against) the claim by providing one or more counter-claims, using the structure for Argumentation we have just reviewed.

When *endorsing* a particular claim or position, you will need to signal that this is the case, with transitions to express addition or exemplification. However, when *rebutting* a particular claim or position, you will need to signal the onset of your Counter-claim with transitions to express contrast.

POSITIVE TRANSITIONS		NEGATIVE TRANSITIONS
Exemplification	**Addition**	**Contrast**
for example	in addition	however
for instance	too	nevertheless
	also	on the other hand
	similarly	in fact
	moreover	actually
	furthermore	
such X	another X, a third X, a similar X, more X, other X	
in one X	other X	

The full format of a Critique now requires:

Global Introduction: an introduction of the topic to which the claim relates

Global Conclusion: a wrap-up, clearly marking the end of the Critique

Overall then, the structure of the Critique is:

Global Introduction

Summary

Evaluation

Global Conclusion

3. Writing a Critique of more than one source: The Persuasive Synthesis

Let us visualize a Critique as follows:

Global Introduction	Summary 1 Evaluation 1	Global Conclusion

Just as an Explanatory Synthesis is a series of Summaries strung together, a Persuasive Synthesis is a series of Summaries and matching Evaluations strung together, within the same frame of Global Introductions and Conclusions.

Global Introduction	Summary 1 Evaluation 1	Summary 2 Evaluation 2	Summary ... Evaluation ...	Global Conclusion

Note that no matter how many items you are critiquing in your Synthesis, you need only one Global Introduction and only one Global Conclusion.

In developing an Explanatory Synthesis, just as in a Critique, you need to help the reader navigate through your text by using clear linking transitions. It is important, for example, that you make clear whether you are

- summarizing a position

OR

- evaluating a position.

When you are evaluating a position, it is important to make clear whether you are

- endorsing the position

OR

- rebutting the position.

Awareness

☑ TASK 5

The following pairs of segments include transitions between different elements of the Critique.

Global Introduction – Summary

Evaluation – Global Conclusion

Try to identify the transition in the space provided. We have done the first example for you.

[1]

> A mouse-sized fossil from China has provided remarkable new insights into the origin of primates.

> At 55 million years old, it represents the earliest known member of this broad group of animals that includes humans.

<u>Global Introduction</u> – <u>Summary</u>

[2]

> Indeed, the American Speech-Language-Hearing Association's Specialty Recognition Program could be expanded to assist us to move in this progressive direction.

> To conclude, current research suggests that in order to meet our legal obligations to the children we serve, we will need to make some changes in our methods of service delivery.

_____________ – _____________

[3]

> It's billed as the world's only known example of a dinosaur stampede – but new research is challenging the established version of events at Lark Quarry, in the Australian outback, almost 100 million years ago.

> Rewind the clocks 95 million years, and imagine the scene…

_____________ – _____________

☑ TASK 6

The following pairs of segments are taken from Critiques. Each pair transitions between a Summary and an Evaluation. Underline the words in the second segment of each pair which (a) indicate a transition and/or (b) evaluate the position presented in the first segment.

We have done the first two examples for you.

Summary – Evaluation

Dr. Wrangham rightly guessed that the leaves had a medicinal purpose—this was, indeed, one of the earliest interpretations of a behaviour pattern as self-medication. His (and everybody else's) assumption was that *Aspilia* contained a drug.

But by the 1990s, chimps across Africa had been seen swallowing the leaves of 19 different species that seemed to have few suitable chemicals in common. The drug hypothesis was looking more and more dubious.

Summary – Evaluation

Many species, for example, consume dirt—a behaviour known as geophagy. Historically, the preferred explanation was that soil supplies minerals such as salt.

But geophagy occurs in areas where the earth is not a useful source of minerals, and also in places where minerals can be more easily obtained from certain plants that are known to be rich in them. Clearly, the animals must be getting something else out of eating earth.

Summary – Evaluation

Dolphins have long been recognised as among the most intelligent of animals but many researchers had placed them below chimps, which some studies have found can reach the intelligence levels of three-year-old children.

Recently, however, a series of behavioural studies has suggested that dolphins, especially species such as the bottlenose, could be the brighter of the two. It has also become clear that they are "cultural" animals…

Summary – Evaluation

> The findings "challenge the foundations of psychology," says Lisa Feldman Barrett, a psychologist and neuroscientist at Northeastern University in Boston.

> Still, says Barrett, the study has limitations. For one, not everyone can afford to own an iPhone, so the study sample may not be representative of the population.

Summary – Evaluation

> The slow pace of Iranian nuclear progress to date strongly suggests that Iran could still need a very long time to actually build a bomb – or could even ultimately fail to do so.

> Indeed, global trends in proliferation suggest that either of those outcomes might be more likely than Iranian success in the near future.

How To

Write a Critique

Make sure that your critique has the following elements:

- A **Global Introduction** to the topic
- A **Summary** of a position or claim
- An **Evaluation** of the position or claim
- A **Global Conclusion**

Write a Persuasive Synthesis

Make sure that your Persuasive Synthesis has the following elements:

- A **Global Introduction** to the topic
- Two or more **Critiques**
- A **Global Conclusion**

ASSIGNMENT

Choose one of the Internet sites below which contains an article on the ethics of animal experimentation. Write a Critique of the article (300–350 words): First, summarize the claim made (or the position taken) by the article and then evaluate that claim negatively. To find material for the Supports for your counter-claim, use some of the responses contained in the reader comments section (these will appear lower down the webpage). To find appropriate material for your *rebuttal*, you will need to skim the comments to see which ones *endorse* the claim made by the article and which argue against, or try to *rebut*, the original claim. Your text should contain all of the elements listed below:

Global Introduction

Summary

- Attribution + Thesis Statement
- Supporting Detail(s)
- Concluding Statement

Evaluation

- Thesis Statement
- Support(s)
- Concluding Statement

Global Conclusion

The following webpages contain both articles on the topic and reader comments:

Can technology help us put an end to animal experimentation?
http://io9.com/5940566/can-technology-help-us-put-an-end-to-animal-experimentation

Animal rights and wrongs
http://www.nature.com/nature/journal/v470/n7335//full/470435a.html

The truth about animal testing
http://www.newstatesman.com/blogs/business/2012/07/truth-about-animal-testing

Animal experiments under the microscope
http://www.abc.net.au/radionational/programs/backgroundbriefing/2013-05-05/4660414

LOGOS, ETHOS, PATHOS, AND LOGICAL FALLACIES

 **UNIT FOCUS**

In this Unit, you will be able to see:

- How the three persuasive strategies of writing **logically**, writing with **credibility**, and writing with **feeling** work in practice when you actually write a text;

- How you can learn to recognize **logical fallacies** in other people's writing and how you can avoid them when you write yourself.

AN INTRODUCTION TO LOGOS, ETHOS, AND PATHOS

- **Logos**, **ethos**, and **pathos** are ancient Greek words, used by a famous Greek philosopher, Aristotle (384–322 BCE), to describe three modes of persuasion, sometimes called **appeals**. The name of each appeal contains a clue as to how it works:

  - **logos**: an appeal to the audience's intellect, using **log**ic and evidence

  - **ethos**: an appeal to the credibility or trustworthiness, demonstrating the personal **eth**ics, of the speaker/writer

  - **pathos**: an appeal to the audience's emotions, creating sym**path**y and em**path**y

☑ TASK 1

Quickly skim through the six boxed text extracts below and determine which is the main mode of persuasion used in each - logos, ethos, or pathos. Then complete the list below.

Extract A ------------------------

Extract B ------------------------

Extract C ------------------------

Extract D ------------------------

Extract E ------------------------

Extract F ------------------------

Extract A

> Let us begin with a simple proposition: What democracy requires is public debate, not information. Of course it needs information too, but the kind of information it needs can be generated only by vigorous popular debate. We do not know what we need to know until we ask the right questions, and we can identify the right questions only by subjecting our ideas about the world to the test of public controversy. Information, usually seen as the precondition of debate, is better understood as its by-product. When we get into arguments that focus and fully engage our attention, we become avid seekers of relevant information. Otherwise, we take in information passively – if we take it in at all.

(Christopher Lasch, "The Lost Art of Political Argument", *Harper's*, September 1990)

☑ TASK 2

1. **Which word in the first clause in the extract suggests that this text will mostly use *logos*?**

   ----

2. **Persuading with a focus on *logos* attempts to ensure that writer and reader will agree. Underline the 6 clauses beginning with *we* which refer to knowing or seeking knowledge.**

3. **In persuasion by means of *logos*, the process of arguing, as a method of knowing the truth of something, is itself important. Underline the words in the extract which refer to argument.**

4. Typically, a writer trying to persuade readers using *logos* is concerned not just with particular objects, events, or people, but with general concepts. Which three general concepts is the extract about?

----

5. Persuasion by *logos* is very often concerned with cause-and-effect relationships. The author of this extract discusses the relationships between democracy, debate, and information, arguing in favor of one particular sequence and against another. Which of the following is the writer proposing and which is he opposing?

Sequence	Cause	Effect	Author's position? [For OR Against]
(a)	**if** there is debate	**then** there will be information	--------------
(b)	**if** there is information	**then** there will be debate	--------------
(c)	**if** there is debate	**then** there will be democracy	--------------
(d)	**if** there is information	**then** there will be democracy	--------------

6. Reflecting the concern of *logos* with cause-and-effect sequences are words relating to conditions governing the causes and effects:

when

otherwise (i.e. if not)

if

However, there are many other ways of expressing cause-and-effect relationships. We show some of them below. Note that the order can be cause-effect or effect-cause.

For each of the relationships expressed below, try to specify whether the cause or the effect is stated first.

X		Y	X = cause OR effect of Y?
democracy	requires	debate	*effect*
it	needs	information too	
information	needs	debate	
the kind of information it needs	can be generated only by	vigorous popular debate	
we can identify the right questions	only by	subjecting our ideas about the world to the test of public controversy	
Information [is] usually seen as	the precondition of	debate	
Information is better understood as [the]	by-product of	debate	

Extract B

My Dear Fellow Clergymen:

While confined here in Birmingham city jail, I came across your recent statement calling my present activities "unwise and untimely."... Since I feel that you are men of genuine good will and that your criticisms are sincerely set forth, I want to try to answer your statement in what I hope will be patient and reasonable terms.

I think I should indicate why I am here in Birmingham, since you have been influenced by the view which argues against "outsiders coming in."... I, along with several members of my staff, am here because I was invited here. I am here because I have organizational ties here.

But more basically, I am in Birmingham because injustice is here. Just as the prophets of the eighth century B.C. left their villages and carried their "thus saith the Lord" far beyond the boundaries of their home towns, and just as the Apostle Paul left his village of Tarsus and carried the gospel of Jesus Christ to the far corners of the Greco-Roman world, so am I compelled to carry the gospel of freedom beyond my own home town. Like Paul, I must constantly respond to the Macedonian call for aid.

(Martin Luther King, Jr., "Letter from Birmingham Jail" open letter, 1963)

☑ TASK 3

1. The personal pronoun which most commonly appeared in Extract A was *we*. What is the personal pronoun which appears most commonly in Extract B?

2. This letter was written during a campaign to obtain civil rights for African Americans. Can you set the following historical events lying behind this text in the most likely chronological order?

Event	Order
Author writes to Birmingham clergymen	-------------------------------
Birmingham clergymen criticize author	-------------------------------
Author campaigns for civil rights in Birmingham	-------------------------------
Author gets arrested and put in Birmingham jail	-------------------------------
Author comes to Birmingham	-------------------------------

In addressing the questions below, try to compose your responses in connected sentences, not just in notes or bullet points.

3. What particular "criticisms" of his own activities is the author responding to?

4. Which words in the first paragraph indicate the kind of character the author hopes to demonstrate?

5. Which words in the first paragraph indicate the kind of personal characteristics the author attributes to his critics?

6. In the third paragraph, the author turns to larger ethical and religious issues. What words does he use to describe these issues?

7. The author compares himself and his actions to a historical and religious figure. Who is this figure, and in what way do you think the author's actions are like his?

8. Who do you think is the intended audience for this text? Why do you think the author likens himself to a religious figure – rather than, say, to a political or military figure?

Note: *Ethos* is important because when we trust a speaker/writer, we are more willing to listen to what they have to say. We trust our doctors and lawyers, for example, even when we do not really understand all of the medical or legal reasoning (*logos*) behind their advice. *Ethos* is an important persuasive strategy in situations in which the speaker/writer cannot assume the trust of the audience.

You may have noted that Extract B also uses *pathos*.

9. The author was not from the city of Birmingham. Which words does he use to describe the feeling of his critics about this fact?

10. What do you think was his defense against this feeling on the part of his critics?

Extract C

For me, commentary on war zones at home and abroad begins and ends with personal reflections. A few years ago, while watching the news in Chicago, a local news story made a personal connection with me. The report concerned a teenager who had been shot because he had angered a group of his male peers. This act of violence caused me to recapture a memory from my own adolescence because of an instructive parallel in my own life with this boy who had been shot. When I was a teenager some thirty-five years ago in the New York metropolitan area, I wrote a regular column for my high school newspaper. One week, I wrote a column in which I made fun of the fraternities in my high school. As a result, I elicited the anger of some of the most aggressive teenagers in my high school. A couple of nights later, a car pulled up in front of my house, and the angry teenagers in the car dumped garbage on the lawn of my house as an act of revenge and intimidation.

(James Garbarino, "Children in a Violent World: A Metaphysical Perspective", *Family Court Review*, Vol 36, Issue 3, 1998)

☑ TASK 4

1. **In Extract C, the writer talks about how important his own experience is to his writing as a journalist. Try to identify all of the phrases which relate to:**

   (a) his personal history

   (b) memory

   (c) emotion

Note: *Pathos* works in persuasion by causing the reader (or hearer) to empathize and sympathize with the writer (or speaker). Once the reader does this, and reader and writer have shared a common emotional response, the writer's hope is that the reader will be more likely to agree with the writer's point of view, or thesis. A common example of this strategy is when public speakers open with a joke: the shared experience of laughing breaks the ice and helps the audience identify with the speaker. Note that writers can, like literary authors, try to arouse any human emotion – love, fear, pity, guilt, shame, pride, hate, or joy – as a way to establish shared emotion and empathy.

2. **What emotions do you think the text extracts below are trying to arouse in the reader?**

Extract D

> Clefts are a major problem in developing countries where there are millions of children who are suffering with unrepaired clefts. Most cannot eat or speak properly. Aren't allowed to attend school or hold a job. And face very difficult lives filled with shame and isolation, pain and heartache. Their clefts usually go untreated because they are poor – too poor to pay for a simple surgery that has been around for decades.

http://www.smiletrain.org/

Emotions: ---------------------------------------

Extract E

> Driving pleasure. It starts the second you set eyes on the sculpted curves of the bodywork. Your heart starts to race, anticipating the exhilaration to come. And when you get behind the wheel and embrace the soft leather seats, the promise of excitement becomes a reality.

http://www.bmw.co.uk/en/topics/discover-bmw/driving-pleasure.html

Emotions: ---------------------------------------

Extract F

> If you died today, who would take care of your family? Would your children be able to go to college without your assistance? Would your spouse or partner be able to retire one day? Though these can be unsettling thoughts to consider, they are essential for anyone who has dependents. A life insurance policy will take care of your loved ones' financial needs after you die.

http://www.lowerrates.com/life-insurance.php

Emotions: ---------------------------------------

CONTEXT

1. Think about the following statement: "Medical research depends on using live animals in experiments." If you asked your friends and family about this claim, do you think they would

    (a) agree?

    (b) disagree?

2. Why do you think there could be general agreement that "Medical research depends on using live animals in experiments"?

3. If we were to carry out some good research on this issue, what results do you think it would show?

    (a) That there are better, cheaper alternatives to using animals for medical research.

    (b) That there are no cheaper or better alternatives to using animals for medical research.

    (c) That there are better alternatives to using animals for medical research but they are more expensive.

4. For the sake of argument, let's assume that research found (b) above to be the case. What kind of data (evidence, examples) and research do you think would support 3(b)?

    (a) Testing a drug on animals, testing it on an alternative (e.g. a computer simulation), then testing it on humans, and comparing all three results.

    (b) Testing a drug on animals, then on an alternative (e.g. a computer simulation), and comparing the results.

    (c) Testing a drug on humans, then on an alternative (e.g. a computer simulation), and comparing the results.

5. Assuming that 4(a) is the correct answer, which of the following do you think is the most plausible conclusion for the research:

    (a) That so-called "alternatives" are not technologically advanced enough to completely replace a living animal in studies.

    (b) That so-called "alternatives" are so technologically advanced that they can completely replace a living animal in studies.

    (c) That so-called "alternatives" are too technologically advanced to completely replace a living animal in studies.

WORDS IN CONTEXT

Using a dictionary if necessary, make sure you understand each word in bold and check the box before moving to the next item.

being the target of a **campaign** (*series of actions*)	☐
proclaiming (*announcing*)	☐
launched an **assault** (*attack*) on	☐
PETA **switched** (*changed*) tactics.	☐
call to arms (*call to action*)	☐
action alerts (*calls to action*)	☐
pointed **disciples** (*followers*) directly	☐
animal-rights **activists** (*campaigners*)	☐
take issue (*disagree*) with	☐
objections (*complaints*) did flow in	☐
to **voice** (*make public*) their complaints	☐
by the hundreds (*in large quantities*)	☐
ranged (*varied*) from **pleas** (*begging*) to curses	☐
outright (*undisguised*) threats of violence	☐
receives their **venom** (*snake poison*)	☐
sling the words (*make the accusation*) "torturer" and "torture"	☐
lacking any soul (*being inhuman*)	☐
a torturer of **helpless** (*weak*) creatures	☐
waste of **taxpayer** (*public*) money	☐
a **life form** (*creature*) slightly above **pond scum** (*micro-organism*)	☐
on the evolutionary tree (*low life form*)	☐
doing science (*carrying out experiments*)	☐
long-running (*taking years*) series of experiments	☐

cellular (*microscopic*) causes of ☐

often-fatal **arrhythmias** (*irregular beat*) in the heart ☐

figuring out how to **thwart** (*stop*) them ☐

expensive and **labor-intensive** (*requiring a lot of work or workers*) to maintain ☐

senior **communications officer** (*public relations person*) ☐

respond to **the masses** (*the general public*) ☐

running (*managing*) the university ☐

public institutions (*government and non-profit organizations*) ☐

have an obligation (*be morally required*) to ☐

There is also the **hitch** (*problem*) that ☐

are far **inferior to** (*worse than*) ☐

negate (*wipe out*) any value ☐

rodents (*rat family*), cats, and **primates** (*ape family*) ☐

"**first cousins**" (*close relatives*) ☐

THE TEXT: PART 1

Now you are ready to read the text.

a. First, skim through the whole text to get the general idea (or gist) of what the text is about.

b. Then read the text as broken down into sections, answering the questions. (Some multiple-choice items may have more than one correct answer.)

Animal Research: Activists' Wishful Thinking, Primitive Reasoning

Letter-writing campaigns may ease consciences, but they won't cure diseases.

Advertising experts know that if you repeat a message often enough, people will believe it, regardless of whether it's truthful or not. **Repetition, we're told, is much more important than accuracy.**

Given that, looking back at weeks of being the target of a campaign this summer by PETA (People for the Ethical Treatment of Animals), I could easily have started believing that I am a satanic monster, lacking any soul, a torturer of helpless creatures, a waster of taxpayer money, and a life form slightly above pond scum on the evolutionary tree.

My new identity emerged when PETA issued another one of its "action alerts" in August, proclaiming "Live Dogs Abused in Heart Attack Tests in OSU Laboratory," perhaps the third or fourth time it has launched an assault on a long-running series of experiments at Ohio State University **investigating** the cellular causes of often-fatal arrhythmias in the heart, with the goal of **figuring out** how to thwart them.

During past campaigns, PETA directed people to write a particular researcher or the university president to voice their complaints. And when those objections did flow in by the hundreds, they were rerouted to me, the contents never seen by the intended recipients. As the senior communications officer for research at my university, my job is to explain the work our scientists do. And when people take issue with some of our studies, I'm the one who receives their phone calls and their **venom**.

Understandably, callers opposed to our work were probably angered by not being able to reach those they had addressed in the past. **But** it's equally understandable that scientists need to keep doing science, and the president needs to keep running the university.

This time, PETA switched tactics. In its call to arms, the organizers pointed disciples directly at me, offering my e-mail address, office phone number, and even a link to my Facebook page as avenues of dissent.

Ten days into the protest, the complaints exceeded 1,100 and ranged from pleas to curses to accusations and outright threats of violence. Letters, e-mails, and Facebook messages exceeded 4,000, and I personally responded to more than 3,000 of them. Public institutions do, after all, have an obligation to respond to the masses. So if one of PETA's goals was to hand a university official some unexpected "busy work," it succeeded.

But if the hope was to halt the research in question, the efforts were wasted.

The reason is simple: Research universities use animals to do their research, and we are OK with that. (There is also the hitch that the Food and Drug Administration requires that drugs and procedures be studied using animals before they can be approved for use by humans.) **While** animal-rights activists often argue that computer simulations or tissue cultures, for example, should be used instead of animals, they neglect to point out that those so-called "alternatives" are too technologically unsophisticated to completely replace a living animal in studies. The data derived from such options are far inferior to those arising from animal use.

And herein lies **the first of several failures of logic** driving those opposed to animal use in research.

Animals actually complicate research. They're expensive and labor-intensive to maintain. If equivalent alternatives were readily available for researchers, scientists would have made the switch long ago. Sadly, effective alternatives are still a wish for the future.

Others **argue** the **alleged wastefulness** of using animals—that the differences between humans and animals negate any value in using animals for research. But decades of research have shown strong similarities between animal models and humans in the way their biological systems work.

Pigs are clearly not humans, but heart valves in both species are nearly interchangeable. Some viruses that attack rodents, cats, and primates can do the same damage to humans. And diseases in some species have highly similar "first cousins" that affect people. The key issue for researchers is that the biological mechanisms for many human and animal viruses are highly similar, if not the same. So understanding how to stop one form of virus in humans can provide the key to doing the same for animals, and vice versa....

(Earle Holland (Assistant Vice President for Research Communications at Ohio State University) , *The Chronicle of Higher Education*, November 7, 2010)

Animal Research: Activists' Wishful Thinking, Primitive Reasoning

Does this Title suggest to you that the writer wishes to emphasize
(a) logic?
(b) his personal character?
(c) emotions?

Letter-writing campaigns may ease consciences, but they won't cure diseases.

This Lead Summary makes two assertions about letter-writing campaigns:
(a) They ease consciences.
(b) They won't cure diseases.

Which assertion does the writer choose to emphasize?

[1] Advertising experts know that if you repeat a message often enough, people will believe it, regardless of whether it's truthful or not. **Repetition, we're told, is much more important than accuracy.**

Does the writer believe and want us to believe that *repetition ... is much more important than accuracy*? How can you tell?

Is the appeal made in this paragraph primarily
(a) logos (logic)?
(b) ethos (credibility)?
(c) pathos (emotions)?

[2] Given that, looking back at weeks of being the target of a campaign this summer by PETA (People for the Ethical Treatment of Animals), I could easily have started believing that I am a satanic monster, lacking any soul, a torturer of helpless creatures, a waster of taxpayer money, and a life form slightly above pond scum on the evolutionary tree.

Is the appeal in this paragraph primarily
(a) logos?
(b) ethos?
(c) pathos?

Which words cause you to think this?

----

[3] My new identity emerged when PETA issued another one of its "action alerts" in August, proclaiming "Live Dogs Abused in Heart Attack Tests in OSU Laboratory," perhaps the third or fourth time it has launched an assault on a long-running series of experiments at Ohio State University **investigating** the cellular causes of often-fatal arrhythmias in the heart, with the goal of **figuring out** how to thwart them.

> ***investigating…figuring out***: Is the motive for including this information about the purpose of the research
> (a) logos?
> (b) ethos?
> (c) pathos?
>
> **Explain how.**

[4] During past campaigns, PETA directed people to write a particular researcher or the university president to voice their complaints. And when those objections did flow in by the hundreds, they were rerouted to me, the contents never seen by the intended recipients. As the senior communications officer for research at my university, my job is to explain the work our scientists do. And when people take issue with some of our studies, I'm the one who receives their phone calls and their **venom**.

> ***venom***: Do you think this metaphorical description of what the campaigners communicate is an appeal to
> (a) logic?
> (b) the credibility of the author?
> (c) emotion?
>
> **If (c), what kind of emotion?**

[5] **Understandably**, callers opposed to our work were probably angered by not being able to reach those they had addressed in the past. **But** it's equally understandable that scientists need to keep doing science, and the president needs to keep running the university.

> ***Understandably***: Does this opening to a description of the callers' behavior appeal to
> (a) logic?
> (b) the trustworthiness of the author?
> (c) emotion?

[6] This time, PETA switched tactics. In its call to arms, the organizers pointed disciples directly at me, offering my e-mail address, office phone number, and even a link to my Facebook page as avenues of dissent.

> ***But…***: Does this sentence appeal to
> (a) logic?
> (b) the trustworthiness of the author?
> (c) emotion?

[7] Ten days into the protest, the complaints exceeded 1,100 and ranged from pleas to curses to accusations and outright threats of violence. Letters, e-mails, and Facebook messages exceeded 4,000, and I personally responded to more than 3,000 of them. Public institutions do, after all, have an obligation to respond to the masses. So if one of PETA's goals was to hand a university official some unexpected "busy work," it succeeded.

Is the appeal in this paragraph primarily
(a) logos?
(b) ethos?
(c) pathos?
(d) all three strategies?

Explain how.

[8] But if the hope was to halt the research in question, the efforts were wasted.

***But if…*: Is the appeal in these sentences primarily**
(a) logos?
(b) ethos?
(c) pathos?

[9] **The reason** is simple: Research universities use animals to do their research, and we are OK with that. (There is also the hitch that the Food and Drug Administration requires that drugs and procedures be studied using animals before they can be approved for use by humans.) **While** animal-rights activists often argue that computer simulations or tissue cultures, for example, should be used instead of animals, they neglect to point out that those so-called "alternatives" are too technologically unsophisticated to completely replace a living animal in studies. The data derived from such options are far inferior to those arising from animal use.

Does *the reason* refer to
(a) why the PETA campaign succeeded?
(b) why the PETA campaign failed?

***While…*: Does this conjunction introduce**
(a) a claim?
(b) a counter-claim?
(c) both claim and counter claim?

Is the appeal in this paragraph primarily
(a) logos?
(b) ethos?
(c) pathos?

[10] And herein lies **the first of several failures of logic** driving those opposed to animal use in research.

> ***the first of several failures of logic:*** **Is the writer here signaling that in the remaining paragraphs he will provide**
> (a) a critique of just one position held by animal activists?
> (b) a critique of several positions held by animal activists?

[11] **Animals actually complicate research.** They're expensive and labor-intensive to maintain. If equivalent alternatives were readily available for researchers, scientists would have made the switch long ago. Sadly, effective alternatives are still a wish for the future.

> ***Animals actually complicate research:*** **Which word indicates that the author is rebutting another position?**
>
> **Which position is the writer trying to rebut?**
> (a) Animals make medical research easier.
> (b) Animals make medical research more difficult.
>
> **Is the appeal in this paragraph**
> (a) logos?
> (b) ethos?
> (c) pathos?
> (d) all three strategies?
>
> **Explain how.**

[12] Others **argue** the **alleged wastefulness** of using animals—that the differences between humans and animals negate any value in using animals for research. But decades of research have shown strong similarities between animal models and humans in the way their biological systems work.

> **Which word here strongly signals that the author is again rebutting a position?**
> (a) *argue*
> (b) *alleged*
> (c) *wastefulness*

[13] Pigs are clearly not humans, but heart valves in both species are nearly interchangeable. Some viruses that attack rodents, cats, and primates can do the same damage to humans. And diseases in some species have highly similar "first cousins" that affect people. The key issue for researchers is that the biological mechanisms for many human and animal viruses are highly similar, if not the same. So understanding how to stop one form of virus in humans can provide the key to doing the same for animals, and vice versa....

Which thesis from the previous paragraph are the details given here supporting?

(a) *...the differences between humans and animals negate any value in using animals for research.*

(b) *...decades of research have shown strong similarities between animal models and humans in the way their biological systems work.*

DID YOU GET THAT?

Title

- ☐ (a) logic: *wishful thinking* sounds like emotion clouding reason, and *primitive reasoning* sounds like bad, oversimplified argument.

Lead Summary

- ☐ (b) They won't cure diseases: The *but* construction lays emphasis on curing disease. Notice how *different* the emphasis becomes if the order is reversed – *Letter-writing campaigns won't cure diseases, but they may ease consciences.*

Paragraph [1]

- ☐ ***repetition is…much more important than accuracy***: The words *we're told* and our own experience suggest that the writer is being ironic and does not want us to believe this statement.

- ☐ **appeal**: (a) logos: There is no reference to emotion or the author.

Paragraph [2]

- ☐ **appeal**: (c) pathos: The author's use of the word *target* invites us to sympathize with him being told that he is *a satanic monster*, etc.

Paragraph [3]

- ☐ ***investigating…figuring out***: (b) ethos. In this article the author identifies with his employer, *Ohio State University*, and this information establishes that the University's experiment have a noble purpose, *how to thwart* heart disease.

Paragraph [4]

- ☐ ***venom***: (c) emotion.

- ☐ sympathy for the writer being the target or victim of hate-mail from the PETA activists.

Paragraph [5]

- ☐ ***Understandably***: (b) the trustworthiness of the author. Even when provoked by the activists' accusations, the author shows that he is reasonable enough to *understand* their anger.

Paragraph [6]

- ☐ ***But…***: (a) logic: Just as he understands the activists, the author is suggesting that they need to understand *that scientists need to keep doing science, and the president needs to keep running the university*.

Paragraph [7]

☐ **appeal**: (d) all three strategies

Explain how.

☐ logos: The final sentence is a classic logical statement, laying out in an orderly way a conclusion (*So...*) and a conditional conclusion (*if... it succeeded*).

☐ ethos: The author shows how fully Ohio State University and he particularly fulfilled their *obligation to respond to the masses.*

☐ pathos: *Curses...accusations and outright threats* are clearly not pleasant to receive, and we are invited to sympathize with their *target*, the writer.

Paragraph [8]

☐ ***But if...***: (a) logos. This conditional conclusion contrasts with the one at the end of the previous paragraph. As before, the *But...* structure emphasizes this second conclusion over the first, implying that indeed *the efforts were wasted.*

Paragraph [9]

☐ ***the reason***: (b) why the PETA campaign failed. This is assumed from the previous sentence and is confirmed in this sentence – despite the complaints, *research universities... are OK with* using animals for research.

☐ ***While*** introduces (c) both claim and counter-claim. *While* indicates a contrast between two situations. In this case, one situation relates to a claim and the other to a related counter-claim:

			[Claim]
Situation 1	activists often argue	that	alternatives should be used
			[Counter-claim]
Situation 2	activists neglect to point out	that	alternatives are too unsophisticated

☐ **appeal**: (a) logos: This paragraph is confined to technical issues.

Paragraph [10]

☐ ***the first of several failures of logic***: (b) a critique of several positions held by animal activists: *the first of* and *several* imply that the other failures of logic will be listed.

Paragraph [11]

☐ ***Animals actually complicate research***: The word *actually* is a transition of contrast, suggesting a rebuttal.

☐ **position**: (a) Animals make medical research easier.

☐ **appeal**: (d) all three strategies

Explain how.

- [ ] logos: Note the cause-and-effect *If...then* structure.

- [ ] ethos: Scientists only use animals because effective alternatives are not readily available; they *wish* alternatives were available and will use them when they are, in the *future*.

- [ ] pathos: *Sadly*... shows that the author and the scientists he is defending share the activists' sadness that animals have to be used.

Paragraph [12]

- [ ] (b) **alleged** shows that the proposition that animal research is *wasteful* is questioned. The transition *But* goes on to fully rebut the proposition.

Paragraph [13]

- [ ] **Which thesis...?**: (b) *...decades of research have shown strong similarities between animal models and humans in the way their biological systems work* is the general thesis (from Para 12) supported by these detailed examples.

LOGICAL FALLACIES

Use of logos involves making a logical **argument**. Although in everyday language an argument can mean a disagreement, in logic an argument means an attempt to persuade by giving reasons for accepting a particular conclusion. The reasons for an argument are separate propositions which are known as **premises.** Here is an example:

Premise 1   This car park is for staff.

Premise 2   I am a member of staff.

Conclusion   I am allowed to park my car in this park.

Not all arguments, however, are logical: forms of argument which are recognized to be invalid or faulty fall into various categories, often described as **logical fallacies.**

Eight common fallacies are explained below. When you have understood each fallacy, try your hand at rewriting the example text with more convincing logic, in the box marked "Fix it." We have done the first example for you.

Ad Hominem Attack

Attacking your opponents personally, rather than their reasoning. (The Latin phrase *ad hominem* means "at or towards the man.")

> Only nutcases believe the Moon landings were a fraud.

Fix it

People who believe the Moon landings were a fraud need to consider carefully the large amount of technical and historical evidence indicating that they happened.

Either/Or (Black-or-White) Reasoning

Reducing all possible alternatives to only two.

> Unless we ban private cars now, the ozone layer will be irrevocably destroyed.

Fix it

Oversimplification

Attributing complex problems to a single cause.

> Boys don't perform as well in schools as girls because they spend more time gaming.

Fix it

Non-sequitur

Having a premise and a conclusion which do not match. (*Non-sequitur* is Latin for "It does not follow.")

> Japanese people live in houses with paper walls. That's why the Japanese car industry is so successful.

Fix it

Hasty Generalization

Generalizing from a data sample which is either too small or is unrepresentative.

> The Arabs I see in London are very rich. All Arabs must be very rich.

Fix it

Faulty Cause-Effect Relationship or *Post hoc ergo propter hoc*

Assuming that because two events co-occur, one is the cause of the other. (The Latin phrase translates as "After this, therefore because of this.")

> I had muesli for breakfast and aced the quiz. The reason I aced the quiz was that I had muesli for breakfast.

Fix it

Begging the Question or Circular Reasoning

Giving your conclusion as a reason but disguising the fact by using different wording.

> The secret of being a good parent is to raise your kids well.

This is merely another way of saying the more obviously circular "The secret of being a good parent is being a good parent."

Fix it

False Analogy

To make, or draw, an analogy is to note that A is like B. To make a false analogy is to assume that because A is like B in one respect, A must be like B in another respect or in all respects.

> Water is liquid and is good for you to drink. Bleach is also liquid and must therefore be good to drink.

Fix it

WORDS IN CONTEXT: PART 2

Using a dictionary if necessary, make sure you understand each word in bold and check the box before moving to the next item.

growing **exponentially** (*at an increasing speed*)	☐
after all (*despite objections*)	☐
muddy the waters (*complicate the issue*)	☐
inflicting pain on (*causing pain to*)	☐
stringent (*strict*) rules and regulations	☐
The **lure** (*attraction*) of	☐
enticingly (*temptingly*) addictive	☐

THE TEXT: PART 2

In the remainder of the text for this Unit, the writer gives more examples of what he earlier described as *several failures of logic* in the thinking of the animal rights' campaigners; some of these correspond to the logical fallacies described above. As you read the text and the comments below, see if you can identify the logical fallacy the writer is referring to and write its name in the space provided.

Opponents of animal use in research are quick to sling the words "torturer" and "torture" at those who do this work, as if scholars and scientists who've devoted their careers to uncovering the causes and cures of human maladies feel visceral joy in inflicting pain on the animals they use in their experiments. Even aside from the fact that there are stringent rules and regulations restricting the care and use of animals, animal-rights advocates seem all too willing to believe that those who do science are the basest members of humanity.

These advocates want simple answers in a complex world. They see things as black or white: All animal use is wrong. Scientists are sadists. It's like wanting old Chevy carburetors to work in modern-day Volkswagens. But today's cars don't necessarily even have carburetors—modern automobiles are more complex than that. So are biological systems, and our understanding of that complexity seems to be growing exponentially by the week.

The core problem may just lie in the conflict between beliefs and logic. The former is built on commitments of faith, while the latter is rooted in fact. The lure of simple answers, based on strong beliefs, requires no facts and is enticingly addictive. Logic and facts only muddy the waters of belief.

After all, how logical is it to think that complaints directed at a university communications official would stop research aimed at improving human health?

But still, the messages keep coming.

(Earle Holland (Assistant Vice President for Research Communications at Ohio State University), *The Chronicle of Higher Education,* November 7, 2010)

[14] Opponents of animal use in research are quick to sling the words "torturer" and "torture" at those who do this work, as if scholars and scientists who've devoted their careers to uncovering the causes and cures of human maladies feel visceral joy in inflicting pain on the animals they use in their experiments. Even aside from the fact that there are stringent rules and regulations restricting the care and use of animals, animal-rights advocates seem all too willing to believe that those who do science are the basest members of humanity.

> **Here the writer points out that by overlooking researchers' humanitarian objectives (***uncovering the causes and cures of human maladies***) and describing animal researchers as "torturers," his opponents are essentially being abusive, or "name-calling."**
>
> **Fallacy A**

---

[15] These advocates want simple answers in a complex world. They see things as black or white: All animal use is wrong. Scientists are sadists. It's like wanting old Chevy carburetors to work in modern-day Volkswagens. But today's cars don't necessarily even have carburetors—modern automobiles are more complex than that. So are biological systems, and our understanding of that complexity seems to be growing exponentially by the week.

> **According to the writer, the activists ignore the realities of** *a complex world***:**
> 1. Ethically, the *black or white* views of the activists ignore the complexity of the situation.
> 2. Scientifically, the activists ignore the complexity of biological systems.
> 3. Legally, the activists ignore the possibility of alternatives to a complete ban on animal experimentation, such as legal regulation.
>
> **Fallacy B**

---

[16] The core problem may just lie in the conflict between beliefs and logic. The former is built on commitments of faith, while the latter is rooted in fact. The lure of simple answers, based on strong beliefs, requires no facts and is enticingly addictive. Logic and facts only muddy the waters of belief.

[17] After all, how logical is it to think that complaints directed at a university communications official would stop research aimed at improving human health?

Here the writer suggests that there is no link between a premise (1) and a conclusion (2).
1. If we complain (about animal rights) to a communications official
2. Then the university will stop carrying out medical research.

Fallacy

[18] But still, the messages keep coming.

☑ TASK 2

Eleven of the thirteen arguments below contain a logical fallacy. Where there is a fallacy, try to name it in the space provided. We have done the first example for you.

1. A guy smoking a pipe once drove into the back of my father's car; pipe-smokers are dangerous drivers.

Hasty Generalization

2. We should ban social networking sites or young people will be corrupted.

3. The reason it's raining so heavily today is because I forgot to bring my umbrella.

4. Many traffic accidents in the USA are related to alcohol consumption but very few are related to tobacco consumption. Banning alcohol would have a bigger effect on reducing traffic accidents than banning tobacco.

5. To allow the press to keep their sources confidential is very advantageous to the country, since it is highly conducive to the interests of the larger community that private individuals should have the privilege of providing information to the press without being identified.

6. Mary's views on fiscal policy are wrong. She's a very silly person.

7. Barry, an Australian, stole my wallet. Thus, all Australians are thieves.

8. Education cannot prepare men and women for marriage. To try to educate them for marriage is like trying to teach them to swim without letting them go into the water. It cannot be done.

9. All human beings are born with a conscience and Hitler was human, so he must have had a conscience.

10. Tens of thousands of Americans have seen lights in the night sky which they could not identify. The existence of life on other planets is fast becoming a certainty.

11. People who think abortion should be banned have no respect for the rights of women. They treat them as nothing but baby-making machines. That's wrong. Women must have the right to choose.

12. Forcing kids to eat vegetables puts them off vegetables. Forcing kids to smoke cigarettes would put them off smoking.

13. The reason that book is illogical is because it doesn't make sense.

GRAMMAR IN CONTEXT

1. Unreal Conditionals

Look at the *if* clauses in the text. Unlike the *real* conditional sentences we considered in Unit F, these sentences refer to situations which are either *unknown* or *unreal*.

Example	Verb tenses	Meaning
…if one of PETA's goals **was** to hand a university official some unexpected "busy work," it **succeeded**. …if the hope **was** to halt the research in question, the efforts **were wasted**.	*if* condition: simple past consequence: simple past	What is described in the *if* condition is not known for certain.
If equivalent alternatives **were** readily available for researchers, scientists **would have made** the switch long ago.	*if* condition: simple past consequence: conditional future perfect	What is described in the *if* condition is unreal or untrue.

The last sentence is of a type used when the situation described in the conditional clause is known to be impossible or untrue. Some grammar books call this an "unreal" or "hypothetical" conditional. In this example, the conditional relates to the *timeless present*, meaning "at any time up to now."

☑ TASK 3

Now read these hypothetical conditional statements and circle the correct answers (Yes or No) to the questions which follow.

1. If Jim had been told about the safari, he would have arrived earlier.

    (a) Was Jim told about the safari?   Yes / No

    (b) Did he arrive earlier?   Yes / No

2. Sheila would have gone to work if she hadn't hurt her arm.

    (a) Did Sheila go to work?   Yes / No

    (b) Did she hurt her arm?   Yes / No

3. **If his math skills were not so weak, Phil would have become an accountant.**
    (a) Did Phil become an accountant?   Yes / No
    (b) Are Phil's math skills weak?   Yes / No

4. **If William Harvey had not discovered the circulation of the blood, someone else would have.**
    (a) Did William Harvey discover the circulation of the blood?   Yes / No
    (b) Did someone else discover the circulation of the blood?   Yes / No

5. **If water was like other substances, the solid form (ice) would be denser than the liquid and sink rather than float.**
    (a) Is water like other substances?   Yes / No
    (b) Does ice sink rather than float?   Yes / No

Note: The form **were** is often used in the singular instead of **was** to indicate an unreal present or timeless state. Thus, example 5 could read: **If water <u>were</u> like other substances ...**

☑ TASK 4

Now try to change each pair of sentences into a conditional sentence. We have done the first example for you.

1. **Joseph didn't revise for the test. As a result, he failed.**

If Joseph had studied for the test, he would have passed.

2. **Smith has expensive health insurance. As a result, he was able to pay for his complicated surgery.**

3. **The auction house did not X-ray the painting. Thus, they did not discover it was a fake.**

4. **My hired car did not have a GPS. Consequently, I couldn't find the factory.**

5. **Mary invested in a lot of dotcom start-ups. As a result, she lost a lot of her savings.**

----

6. **The hotel doesn't keep up with changing trends. Therefore, it is losing business.**

----

2. *That*: Reporting Propositions

That is a word with many functions in English. Notice what function *that* is serving in the sentences below.

Example	Function of *that*
Advertising experts know **that** if you repeat a message often enough, people will believe it… …animal-rights activists often argue **that** computer simulations or tissue cultures, for example, should be used instead of animals… …they neglect to point out **that** those so-called "alternatives" are too technologically unsophisticated… …willing to believe **that** those who do science are the basest members of humanity.	Introduces an idea or thesis which is being reported

Note: In such cases (and others) it is grammatically possible to omit *that*. However, if you do, there is a risk of temporary ambiguity. Notice how the above versions without *that* are ambiguous until after the last word shown.

Advertising experts know if you repeat a message…

they neglect to point out those so-called "alternatives"…

believe those who do science…

Use of *that* helps us avoid this potential ambiguity by signaling clearly that the writer is reporting a complete proposition. Wanting to avoid ambiguity makes the use of *that* for reporting much more common in academic writing than in ordinary speech or in other kinds of writing.

☑ TASK 5

You may have noticed that there is a great range in the reporting verbs which appear before *that*. The subject of these reporting verbs can be a human being (e.g. a researcher) or some information (e.g. an experiment, a body of literature, or certain data) which is the basis for an interpretation.

Osthaus
The new research ⎱ *suggests that* cats are not as clever as often assumed.

Note that reporting verbs are not all synonyms for *say* or *think* but have different meanings. These often relate to degree of *certainty*, as we indicate below:

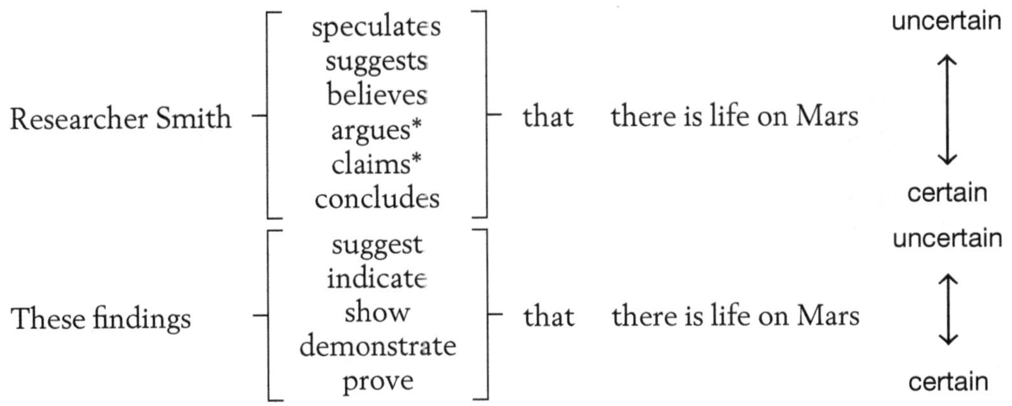

* The verbs *argue* and *claim* are often used by researchers when they know that their argument is likely to be disputed by others.

Now see if you can choose an appropriate reporting verb with the correct tense and person ending for the following sentences. We have done the first example for you.

1. For many years now, scientists ___have believed___ **that** dolphins are very intelligent.

2. Initial evidence in the nineteenth century _________________ **that** dinosaurs were related to present-day lizards.

3. Long before there was any data to support the idea, it was Einstein who first _________________ **that** space and time are not absolute.

4. Many different experiments over decades _________________ conclusively **that** humans cannot teach apes how to talk.

5. Although people tend to think cats are smarter than dogs, on the basis of her string experiments Dr Osthaus _________________ **that** dogs are in fact smarter.

6. New fossil discoveries in Greece _________________ **that** *homo sapiens* may have lived there three hundred thousand years ago.

7. Pasteur was not sure but _________________ **that** food rots because of the unseen activity of microscopic organisms.

TEXT ORGANIZATION

Final notes on Counter-argumentation

As you will remember from previous units, Counter-argumentation is often explicitly marked by transitional expressions.

☑ TASK 6

Underline the transitions expressing contrast in the extracts below, like the *but* we have underlined in the first example shown. These transitions signal that, having stated a particular claim, the author now wishes to argue against it, or to introduce a Counter-claim.

> Understandably, callers opposed to our work were probably angered by not being able to reach those they had addressed in the past. But it's equally understandable that scientists need to keep doing science, and the president needs to keep running the university.
>
> Ten days into the protest, the complaints exceeded 1,100 and ranged from pleas to curses to accusations and outright threats of violence....
>
> But if the hope was to halt the research in question, the efforts were wasted.
>
> The reason is simple: Research universities use animals to do their research, and we are OK with that. ... While animal-rights activists often argue that computer simulations or tissue cultures, for example, should be used instead of animals, they neglect to point out that those so-called "alternatives" are too technologically unsophisticated to completely replace a living animal in studies. The data derived from such options are far inferior to those arising from animal use.
>
> Others argue the alleged wastefulness of using animals—that the differences between humans and animals negate any value in using animals for research. But decades of research have shown strong similarities between animal models and humans in the way their biological systems work.
>
> Pigs are clearly not humans, but heart valves in both species are nearly interchangeable. Some viruses that attack rodents, cats, and primates can do the same damage to humans....

In addition to adding **explicit** signals of Counter-argumentation, writers may introduce counter-claims **implicitly**, that is, without using an explicit connector such as *but* or *however.* They assume that the contrast will be obvious to the reader based on meaning. Notice how the author of this text counter-argues *implicitly* by introducing a contrast between the claims and problems with the claims:

Text	Words indicating a problem with the claim
Too bad they don't always express the same compassion and concern for their fellow humans. This latest campaign against Ohio State, for example, included numerous demands to replace animals in research with human prisoners. ✓**The ethical problem** of that substitution seems to have eluded some animal-rights protesters…	**Too bad**: suggests a problem. **The ethical problem**: confirms the *problem*. ✓ indicates where *but* or *however* could be used to make the counter-claim explicit.

☑ TASK 7

In the text extracts below, the author introduces Counter-argumentation *without* using explicit transitions. See if you can identify the claim or counter-claim in each of the following pairs.

[1] The widely held notion of "common sense" suggests that people believe their categories for thinking about how the world works are a natural reflection of the way the world is. If we look at the sources of these categories, we find that some are natural in origin, but the majority are social.

Claim: *People believe their categories for thinking about the world simply reflect the nature of the world.*

Counter-claim: ____

[2] Denotative meaning, as given in dictionaries, is that kind of meaning which is fully supported by ordinary semantic conventions, such as the convention that *window* refers to a particular kind of aperture in a wall or roof.

Unfortunately, even dictionary definitions of words are not without their problems. This is because they impose a rigidity of meaning that words do not often show once they are put into a context.

Claim: ____

Counter-claim: *The denotative meanings of words often change according to their context.*

[3] Of course, you may fear criticism because you feel you need the love and approval of other people in order to be a worthwhile and a happy person. The problem with this point of view is that you'll have to devote all of your energies to trying to please people, and you won't have much left for creative, productive living. Paradoxically, many people may find you less interesting and desirable than your more self-assured friends.

Claim: _Trying to please other people will make you popular._

Counter-claim: ____

Exposition

☑ TASK 8

Perhaps you will have noticed that the Animal Rights text in this unit is a highly argumentative text which does not contain much Exposition. Nevertheless, there is some Exposition, when the writer reports a sequence of events, as in the following extract:

My new identity emerged when PETA issued another one of its "action alerts" in August, proclaiming, "Live Dogs Abused in Heart Attack Tests in OSU Laboratory," perhaps the third or fourth time it has launched an assault on a long-running series of experiments at Ohio State University…

Underline the main verbs in the following sentences and then decide whether the paragraph from which the sentence is taken is Exposition or Argumentation. We have done the first two examples for you.

1. Advertising experts <u>know</u> that if you <u>repeat</u> a message often enough, people <u>will believe</u> it, regardless of whether it'<u>s</u> truthful or not.

   [_Argumentation_]

2. During past campaigns, PETA <u>directed</u> people to write a particular researcher or the university president to voice their complaints.

   [_Exposition_]

3. Understandably, callers opposed to our work were probably angered by not being able to reach those they had addressed in the past. This time, PETA switched tactics.

   [_____________________]

4. The reason is simple: Research universities use animals to do their research, and we are OK with that.

    [-------------------------------]

5. And herein lies the first of several failures of logic driving those opposed to animal use in research.]

    [-------------------------------]

6. Animals actually complicate research.

    [-------------------------------]

7. Others argue the alleged wastefulness of using animals – that the differences between humans and animals negate any value in using animals for research.

    [-------------------------------]

How To

Use Logos, Ethos, and Pathos

Make sure in your academic writing that:

- Whether or not you decide to use **ethos** and **pathos**, you use **logos**, namely, you appeal to the reasoning powers of your reader;
- You avoid **logical fallacies**.

ASSIGNMENT

Imagine that you have volunteered to spend part of your summer vacation working for an international charity abroad. In order to take part, you must persuade people to donate money to the charity or sponsor you personally.

Write a letter (350–400 words) you could use to send to potential sponsors asking them to support you financially. The letter needs to make logical and emotional appeals (logos and pathos), as well as building trust (ethos) in both you as an individual and the charity you plan to work for.

To give you ideas, here are some websites giving details of charities which undertake construction projects in developing countries:

Go overseas
http://www.gooverseas.com/volunteer-abroad/building-construction

UN Volunteers
https://www.onlinevolunteering.org/en/vol/index.html

United Planet: Volunteer Abroad Construction Programs
http://www.unitedplanet.org/construction-volunteer-abroad

Global Volunteer Network
http://www.globalvolunteernetwork.org/programs/index.php

Projects Abroad
http://www.projects-abroad.com.au/projects/building/

DOCUMENTATION OF SOURCES

UNIT FOCUS

In this Unit, you will be able to see:

■ Why academic writers take great care to **document** all sources used in their writing;

■ How to write a **references list**;

■ How to **cite** sources in your own paper.

THE PURPOSE OF DOCUMENTING SOURCES

As we have tried to show so far, popularized research articles regularly refer to scientists and the institutions where they work, for example, take the *Animal Doctors* text in Unit A:

> For the past decade Dr Engel, **a lecturer in environmental sciences at Britain's Open University,** has been collating examples of self-medicating behaviour in wild animals.

For the newspaper reader, this information is enough and no further documentation is given or expected. However, academic writing is somewhat different. For example, in an academic article which appeared in 2006 in the research journal *Animal Behaviour*, notice how differently Dr. Engel is referred to:

> Most evidence in support of the self-medication hypothesis in animals is anecdotal and equivocal (Clayton & Wolfe 1993; Lozano 1998; **Engel 2002**).
> Under the premise of homeostatic behavior, the distinction between food and medicine is artificial, because ingesting food and medicine is the means to the same end, staying well **(Engel 2002)**.

Discussion Point

Brainstorm with a partner and discuss with your professor what each part of *(Engel 2002)* means and why the writer has put this reference to Engel 2002 at these points in the text.

At the end of the same article, under the list headed "References," the author of the article provides more information:

Engel, C. (2002). *Wild Health*. New York: Houghton Mifflin.

Discussion Point

What does each part of the following reference mean?

Engel, C. (2002). *Wild Health*. New York: Houghton Mifflin.

Why has the writer put this information at the end of the text?

As you may guess, these wordings are highly conventionalized and shortened forms which give readers details of a published text written by the researcher where more information about the research is available.

In this case, the article is directing the reader to a book Dr. Engel wrote entitled *Wild Health* which was published in 2002 by the New York publishing house Houghton Mifflin. This is an example of **documentation,** also known as **referencing** and **citation**.

Before we look in detail at the *How* of documentation, let's think a little about the *Why*. Why bother with documentation?

Discussion Point

Why do academic writers document their sources?

Hint: Think through what might happen if writers did **not** document their sources.

In essence, there are four reasons why academic writers document their sources. These are listed in the first column of the task on the opposite page.

☑ TASK 1

See if you can match each reason with the appropriate paraphrase in the second column.

Reason for citation	What the writer is saying via the citation
1. To boost their own credibility: To persuade using logos, an appeal to evidence, and ethos, an appeal to credibility.	**A: This position (Engel, 2002) is not my idea: I am not claiming anything new here.**
2. To save space: The writers don't need to give details to convince readers who might otherwise be curious or doubtful about a particular point. Writers can focus instead on their own positions.	**B: This position has been held by other people (Engel, 2002). I am going on to agree, modify, or argue against their position.**
3. To distinguish their own position from that of other researchers: This most often happens in a single section of a research paper cevoted to this purpose, often called a **literature review**.	**C: If you want to know more details on this secondary point, you'll find them here (Engel, 2002).**
4. To avoid the appearance of stealing the ideas of others: To claim other people's data, conclusions, or even words, as your own work is known as **plagiarism** (from a Latin word for kidnapping, or man-stealing) and it is a very serious matter. *	**D: You don't have to take my word for it: this other expert has the evidence for this point (Engel, 2002).**

* In academic research, being original – or presenting a New position – is very important. If discovered, plagiarism can lead to professional dishonor and dismissal.

Answers

1. A B C (D)

2. A B C D

3. A B C D

4. A B C D

> **Discussion Point**
>
> You may be wondering whether the above reasons as to why professional academic research writers document sources really apply to *you* as a student writer.
>
> Can you think of any *other* reasons your professors might want you to document your sources?

Citing the writings of others helps your professors as they look for evidence of certain knowledge and skills. These include your ability to:

1. develop a thesis (explanatory or persuasive) which is supported by publicly available evidence

2. integrate the research of others into your writing, in particular to
   - summarize
   - paraphrase
   - quote

3. read and understand what experts have written about your topic, including experts you may disagree with*

4. understand the ethics of research writing and avoid plagiarism

THE TWO COMPONENTS OF DOCUMENTATION SYSTEMS

As we have seen with the Dr Engel example above, there are two *interdependent* components of documentation. Any system of documentation you follow will contain these two components:

- **Full Citation** – the full details of the sources you used (notice the *order* of the elements), e.g.

  Engel, C. (2002). *Wild Health.* New York: Houghton Mifflin.

- **In-Text Citation** – only enough details to allow your reader to locate the full citation, e.g.

  (Engel, 2002)

---

* For this reason, citation is likely to be common in both Explanatory and Persuasive Syntheses.

Note that in the APA citation system, there is a comma before the date in an In-Text Citation. Also note that, in the case of quotations, your In-Text Citation will need to add the number of the page from which you took the quotation, e.g.

（Engel, 2002, p. 73)

This is very important.

> **Discussion Point**
>
> At this point, you may be thinking: Why make life so complicated? Why not just give the full citation of the source where it is referred to in the text?
>
> Can you see any reasons why such a system might be a bad idea?

In the APA system, you list all the Full Citations at the end of the text, which is why they are also called *End-Text Citations*.

Comparison of In-Text and End-Text Citations

Citation	Where?	Why?	How long?	APA example in context
In-Text	in the particular sentences where the source is cited	to point readers, with as little distraction as possible, to the right place in the alphabetic End-Text Citations list	short	premise of homeostatic behavior, the distinction between food and medicine is artificial, because ingesting food and medicine is the means to the same end, staying well (Engel, 2002). However, viewed from within a different etiological perspective, the distinction is possibly valuable, affording *gestalt* insights into animal pathology (De Jong, 2000; Hofmeister, 1998; Joyce, 2003).
End-Text	in an alphabetical list after the text	to give readers the information they would need in order to find the original source themselves, in a library or online	long	Eareckson, J. (2011). Squirrel epidemiology: Ecosystems in action 7(3): 109–127. Engel, C. (2002). *Wild health.* New York: Houghton Mifflin. Grubb, N. (1987). *On the health of species.* London: Eyre and Spottiswood.

Readers of your paper will meet the citations in this order:

1. **In-Text Citation**   2. **End-Text Citation**

Note, however, that as a writer it is best to prepare the citations in this order:

1. **End-Text Citation**   2. **In-Text Citation**

It is a good idea to compile the detailed information you will need for the End-Text Citations as you are writing your paper. This is because it can be difficult to retrieve all of the original information at a later time.

Warning

All referencing systems require a lot of detailed information. Try to avoid the following unfortunate scenario:

The due date to submit your paper has arrived but you find that you cannot remember and have no time to retrace the details of a particular source you have used.

In such a situation, there are only two options, both unsatisfactory:

- Leave out the material you have worked on, wasting the effort already spent on it and leaving a gap in your writing.

- Retain the material but without any documentation, committing plagiarism.

Tips

■ Do not postpone documentation until near the end of writing.

■ Consider the documentation of your paper as a continuing work in progress which starts as soon as you begin working on your paper.

■ Keep a full record of the details of any source you think you might eventually use.

■ Compile a small database of citations as you find sources – ready-made citation software is available from:

- online referencing sites (e.g. Web of Science)

- online library catalogs

- word-processing software (e.g. in MS Word, the "Citations & Bibliography" feature in the References tab).

APA

There are many different systems of documentation, e.g. APA, MLA, Chicago, and Harvard. Each system has very detailed conventions (rather like those in a dictionary) for abbreviating, punctuating, and sequencing information.

As a general rule, the system you use depends on the academic discipline for which you are writing. In this book we use the APA (American Psychological Association) system, which is commonly used within the social sciences, business, and education, and is similar to referencing styles used for the physical sciences.

Official Manual

Publication Manual of the American Psychological Association (6th edition, 2nd printing). Washington, DC: American Psychological Association.

Online Guide

Purdue University Online Writing Lab: http://owl.english.purdue.edu/owl/section/2/

> **Tip**
>
> To save yourself painful discoveries later (e.g. that you do not have the initials of the editor of the volume), check out *in advance* what details are required for APA citations.

We provide below examples of APA conventions for common types of source. For other types of source you will need to consult the official manual or online guides.

In the details given below, note the conventions used in APA for:

- the sequence of information
- abbreviations used
- use of italic font
- punctuation between the various elements (e.g. brackets, commas, periods)
- page numbers for sources and quotations

End-Text Citations in APA

Citations appear in a list after the text under the heading "References."

Although the precise details vary according to the type of source, the basic order in APA is:

1 Author name, initial(s)	2 Date	3 Title	4 Place of publication	5 Publisher
Engel, C.	(2002).	*Wild health.*	New York:	Houghton Mifflin.

Print Sources

Book

Elbow, P. (1998). *Writing with power: Techniques for mastering the writing process* (2nd ed.). Oxford: Oxford University Press.

> **Note:** Only the first word and proper names are capitalized in titles and subtitles of books and articles.

Chapter, article, or essay in an edited book

Bjork, R. A. (1989). Retrieval inhibition. In H. L. Roediger (Ed.), *Varieties of memory and consciousness* (pp. 309–330). Hillsdale, NJ: Erlbaum.

> **Note:** Book titles, but not article titles, are in italic font.

Reference work

Gove, P. B. (Ed.) (2002). *Webster's third new international dictionary of the English language, unabridged.* Springfield, MA: MerriamWebster.

Print journal article

Mottola, E. & Vaulin, R. (2013). More on black holes and quantum information. *Physics Today, 66*(11), 9–10. doi: 10.1063/PT.3.2161

> **Notes:** All key words in a journal title are capitalized, and the title and the volume number (but not the issue number, which is sometimes not included) are in italics. The final abbreviation "doi" stands for Digital Object Identifier and needs to be included in the citation for all articles which have a doi.

Print newspaper article

Bundhun, R. (2013, June 17). Gold imports to India set for record. *The National*, p. B5.

> **Note:** For publications such as newspapers that give the day of publication, this is included within parentheses after the year of publication.

Newspaper article with no author

Rouhani needs to mend ties with Gulf. (2013, June 17). *Gulf News*, p. A24.

Electronic Sources

Online newspaper article

Bundhun, R. (2013, June 17). Gold imports to India set for record. *The National*. Retrieved from http://www.thenational.ae/business/industry-insights/economics/gold-imports-to-india-set-for-record

Blog post

NeverSeconds. (2013, March 24). *Meeting Madam President Dr Banda of Malawi* [Web log post]. Retrieved from http://neverseconds.blogspot.ae/2013/03/meeting-madam-president-dr-banda-of.html

Print journal article retrieved online

Atkins, G. (2013). The Edwardian social network. *History Today*, *63*(6), 38–42. Retrieved from http://www.historytoday.com/guy-atkins/edwardian-social-network

Print journal article retrieved from online database

Bonner, A. (2005). Turkey, the European Union and paradigm shifts. *Middle East Policy*, *12*(1), 44–71. Retrieved from Academic Search Premier database.

Online encyclopedia article

Nomadism. (2013). In *Encyclopædia Britannica*. Retrieved from http://www.britannica.com.ezproxy.aus.edu/EBchecked/topic/417292/nomadism

Website with no author and no date

Traditional architecture. (n.d.). Retrieved from UAE Interact website. http://www.uaeinteract.com/culture/architecture.asp

Note: Date of retrieval may be provided for Internet sources. For example:

Atkins, G. (2013). The Edwardian social network. *History Today*, *63*(6), 38–42. Retrieved on January 11, 2014 from http://www.historytoday.com/guy-atkins/edwardian-social-network

Other Sources

TV broadcast

Rees, L. (Producer). (2001, October 5). *The war of the century, Part 1: Scorched earth* [Television broadcast]. London: British Broadcasting Corporation.

Video online

TED (Producer). (2012, March). *Susan Cain: The power of introverts* [Video file]. Retrieved from http://www.ted.com/talks/susan_cain_the_power_of_introverts.html

Personal communication

Not listed as an end-text reference.

In-Text Citations in APA

Author surname and year of publication are used. Notice that while the year of publication always appears in parentheses, the author's name may or may not appear within the same parentheses:

> Plant-derived immunomodulatory compounds have been used in traditional remedies for both humans and animals (Engel, 2002), but critically assessing their effectiveness and understanding their mechanisms of action are in their infancy.

Alternatively, the author name may appear in a narrative outside the parentheses.

> Engel (2002) approached this subject by exploring behaviors of wild animals and how they manage internal parasites.

A secondary function of In-Text Citations is to help the reader by indicating the exact place in the source to which the current writer is referring. If you are directly **quoting** a source, you are obliged to give the page number (single page numbers are abbreviated as "p." and multiple numbers as "pp.").

> As Engel (2002) suggests, "A domestic cat chewing grass (or house plants) may be trying to self-medicate" (p. 217).

Notice that citation parentheses appear before the end, or period, of a sentence. An exception to this rule is for direct quotations of 40 words or more, which are placed in a free-standing block, indented and without quotation marks:

> Engel (2002) warns about the danger of assuming intentionality:
>
> > In the study of animal behavior, intentional language is often used, as it is less cumbersome than repeatedly using long-winded evolutionary explanations. We might say, for example, that males compete for females in order to produce more offspring than other males; but biologists do not really think that males *intend* in any conscious or deliberate way to produce the most offspring. (pp. 36–37)

If there is no named author, the first item in the End-Text Citation takes its place and will also be used in the In-Text Citation; this is usually the title of the article.

> Initial reaction in the Gulf suggests that the new president will need to "reverse Ahmedinejad's policies" to reassure Arab states ("Rouhani needs to mend ties with Gulf," 2013).

If no date is available in the End-Text Citation, the abbreviation "n.d." takes its place in the In-Text Citation:

> Among the most important considerations in the layout of traditional UAE housing were privacy and ventilation ("Traditional architecture," n.d.)

Personal communications can be referred to in two ways:

> The importance of habit formation in language development had been underestimated (Noam Chomsky, personal communication, September 13, 2010).

> Chomsky believed that the importance of habit formation in language development had been underestimated (personal communication, September 13, 2010).

LOCATING CITATION INFORMATION

For **online** sources, all of the information you need should be readily available from the pages themselves or other pages which link to them.

For **print** sources, you will need to find the information for yourself:

Books: the title page and its reverse

Articles: head and/or possibly foot of page

☑ TASK 2

For each of the sources illustrated on the following pages, compile an End-Text Citation in APA format in the space provided. We have done the first example for you.

1. Book

Cover

Reverse of title page

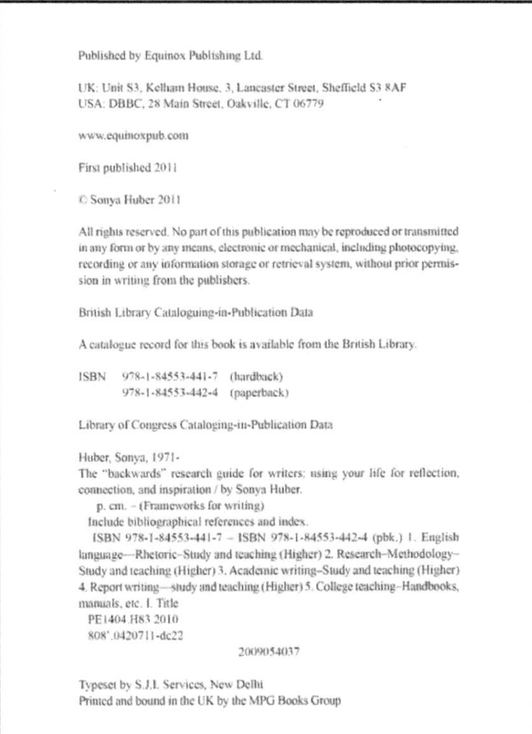

Published by Equinox Publishing Ltd.

UK: Unit S3, Kelham House, 3, Lancaster Street, Sheffield S3 8AF
USA: DBBC, 28 Main Street, Oakville, CT 06779

www.equinoxpub.com

First published 2011

© Sonya Huber 2011

All rights reserved. No part of this publication may be reproduced or transmitted in any form or by any means, electronic or mechanical, including photocopying, recording or any information storage or retrieval system, without prior permission in writing from the publishers.

British Library Cataloguing-in-Publication Data

A catalogue record for this book is available from the British Library.

ISBN   978-1-84553-441-7   (hardback)
        978-1-84553-442-4   (paperback)

Library of Congress Cataloging-in-Publication Data

Huber, Sonya, 1971-
The "backwards" research guide for writers: using your life for reflection, connection, and inspiration / by Sonya Huber.
    p. cm. – (Frameworks for writing)
  Include bibliographical references and index.
    ISBN 978-1-84553-441-7 – ISBN 978-1-84553-442-4 (pbk.) 1. English language—Rhetoric–Study and teaching (Higher) 2. Research–Methodology–Study and teaching (Higher) 3. Academic writing–Study and teaching (Higher) 4. Report writing—study and teaching (Higher) 5. College teaching–Handbooks, manuals, etc. I. Title
  PE1404.H83 2010
  808'.0420711-dc22
                        2009054037

Typeset by S.J.I. Services, New Delhi
Printed and bound in the UK by the MPG Books Group

End-Text Citation

Huber, S. (2011). *The backwards research guide for writers: Using your life for reflection, connection and inspiration.* Sheffield, UK, and Oakville, CT: Equinox.

2. Journal Article

From first page

Applied Linguistics 2013: 34/2: 173–190   © Oxford University Press 2012
doi:10.1093/applin/ams038   Advance Access published on 9 August 2012

Western Perceptions of Hong Kong Ten Years On: A Corpus-driven Critical Discourse Study

[1,]*WINNIE CHENG and [2,][†]PHOENIX W. Y. LAM

[1]Department of English, The Hong Kong Polytechnic University, Hung Hom, Hong Kong, and [2]Department of English Language and Literature, Hong Kong Baptist University, Kowloon Tong, Hong Kong
*E-mail: egwcheng@polyu.edu.hk, [†]E-mail: engplam@hkbu.edu.hk

This article studies the Western perceptions of and relations with Hong Kong a decade after the reversion of the sovereignty from Britain to China in 1997. Previous studies have demonstrated that the West had a significantly negative view on the future of Hong Kong with respect to the handover. According to recent observations, however, the perceptions of the West have undergone a noticeable change. This article aims at investigating the West's understanding, opinions and positions regarding Hong Kong today compared with those in

End-Text Citation

3. Chapter in Edited Book

From an online library catalog entry for a book – write the citation for Chapter 2 (boxed)

<table>
<tr><td>Title</td><td colspan="3">New perspectives on CALL for second language classrooms / edited by Sandra Fotos, Charles Browne.</td></tr>
<tr><td>Publisher</td><td colspan="3">Mahwah, N.J. : L. Erlbaum Associates, 2004.</td></tr>
<tr><td></td><td>LOCATION</td><td>CALL #</td><td>STATUS</td></tr>
<tr><td></td><td>General - 2nd Fl</td><td>P53.28 .N485 2004</td><td>AVAILABLE</td></tr>
</table>

Description xi, 357 p. : ill. ; 24 cm.

Series ESL and applied linguistics professional series

Summary "This handbook is designed to help language teachers, teacher trainers, and students team more about their options for using computer-assisted language learning (CALL) and develop an understanding of the theory and research supporting these options." "The book does not require prior knowledge of CALL, computers, or software." "By integrating theoretical issues, research findings, and practical guidelines on different aspects of CALL, this book offers teachers multiple levels of resources for their own professional development, for needs-based creations of specific CALL activities, for curriculum design, and for implementation of institutional and inter-institutional CALL projects."--BOOK JACKET.

Bibliog. Includes bibliographical references and indexes.

Subject Language and languages -- Computer-assisted instruction.

Alt Author Fotos, Sandra.

Browne, Charles.

ISBN 080584404X (cloth : alk. paper)

0805844058 (pbk. : alk. paper)

Table of Contents

I	Introduction to CALL	1
1	The development of CALL and current options / Sandra Fotos , Charles Browne	3
2	Technological change and the future of CALL / Mark Warschauer	15
3	The new language centers and the role of technology : new mandates, new horizons / Peter Liddell , Nina Garrett	27
II	Perspectives on classroom CALL	41
4	Learner training for effective use of CALL / Philip Hubbard	45
5	Electronic media in second language writing : an overview of tools and research findings / Martha C. Pennington	69

End-Text Citation

4. Website
Accessed today

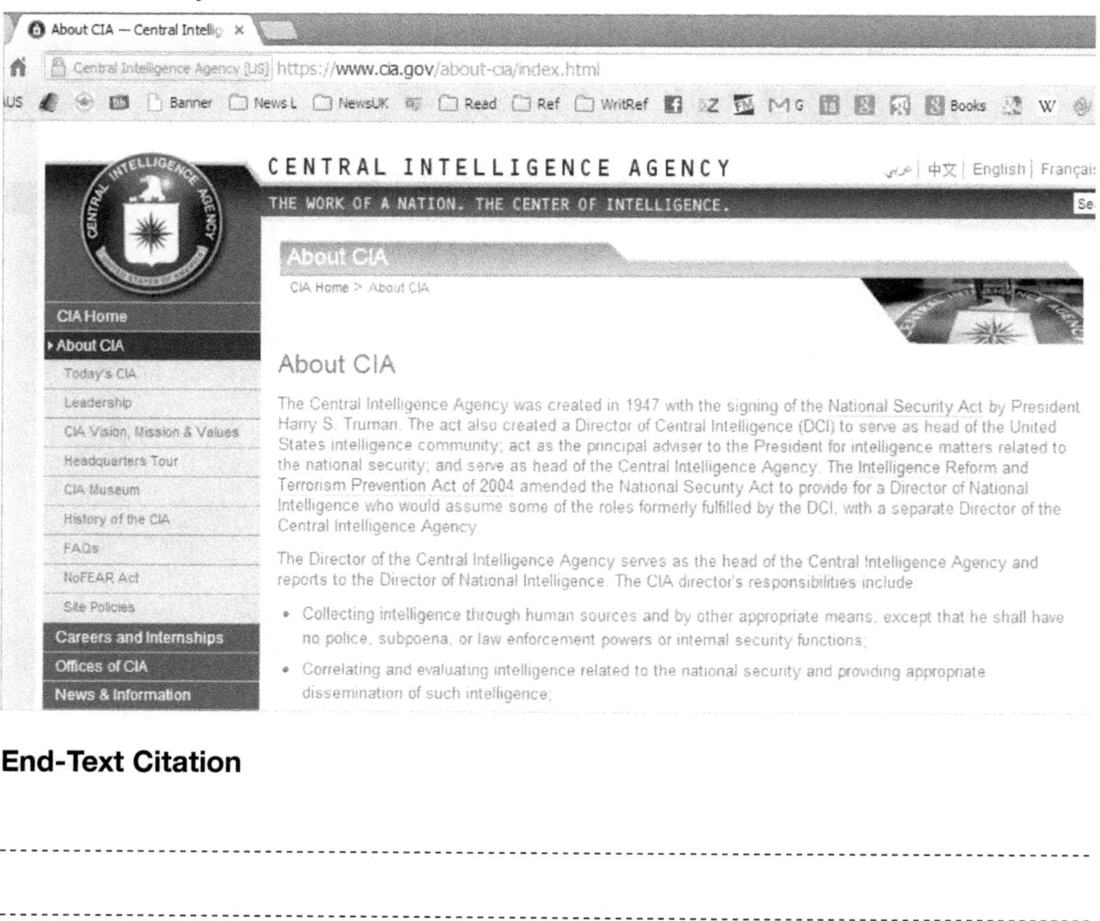

End-Text Citation

5. Unsigned Newspaper Editorial

Cutting from section A, page 8, of the Gulf News *of October 28, 2006*

End-Text Citation

6. Blog Post

Posted on 06/21/2013 by Juan Cole

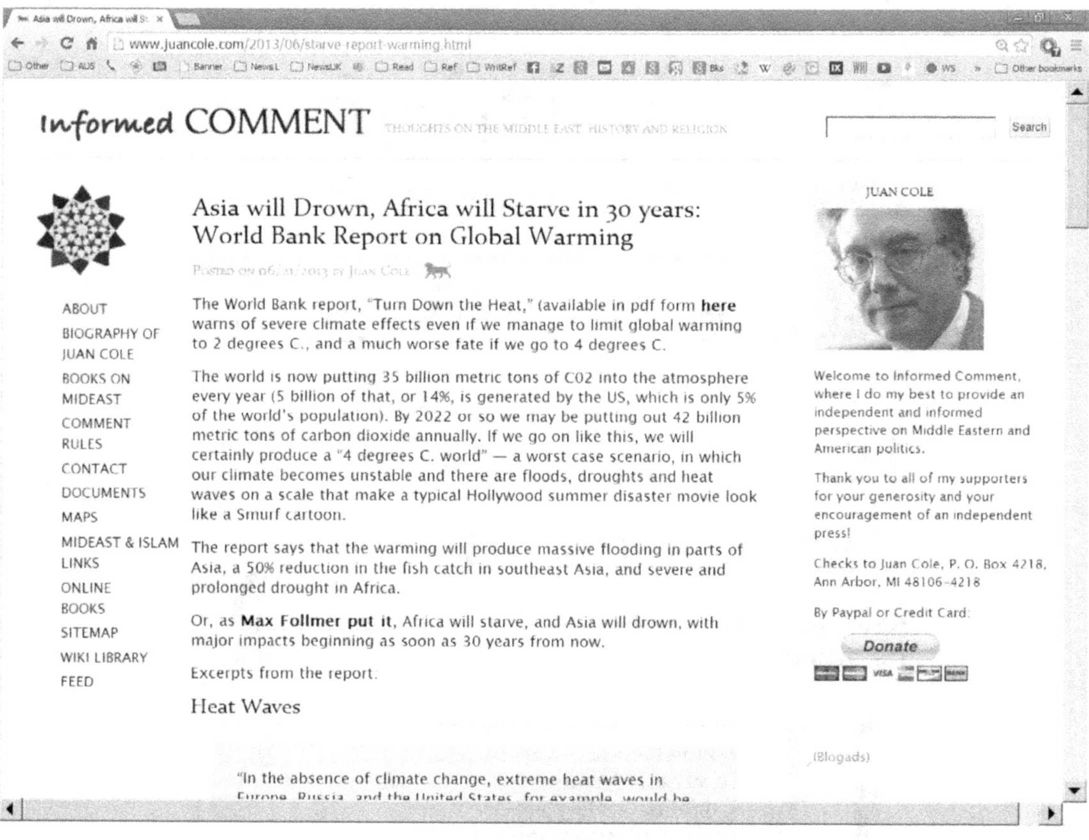

End-Text Citation

☑ TASK 3

Imagine you are working on a research paper related to the use of the English language around the world. From the information in the box below, compile on a separate sheet of paper a list of End-Text Citations according to the documentation system used in your major subject or in APA format. Give the list its correct title and format the citations according to that system.

Source A

Quotation from page 3 of the script of a play entitled *Pygmalion*, written by George Bernard Shaw, as it appears in the version published in 2000 by Penguin Books of London, UK.

Source B

Quotation from page 1 of the second edition of a book entitled *A Practical Introduction to Phonetics*, written by John C. Catford and published in 2001 by Oxford University Press of Oxford, UK.

Source C

Information from a book chapter entitled "Sociolinguistics in the British Isles," written by Jane Stuart-Smith and Bill Haddican. The chapter occupies pages 296–309 of a book entitled *The Routledge Handbook of Sociolinguistics around the World* edited by Martin J. Ball and published in 2010 by Routledge in New York City.

Source D

Paraphrase of information from an anonymous article entitled "David and Victoria Beckham 'getting posher', study finds" appearing on the BBC News website, dated 17 April 2013, at this URL: http://www.bbc.co.uk/news/uk-england-22179969.

Source E

Information from an article entitled "Two thousand million?" written by David Crystal, appearing on pages 3–6 of Volume 24, Issue 1, of the journal entitled *English Today* published in March 2008.

☑ TASK 4

Note the differences between the placing of the name of the source in these two versions of a citation:

(a) As Engel (2002) suggests, "A domestic cat chewing grass (or house plants) may be trying to self-medicate" (p. 217).

(b) It has been suggested that "[a] domestic cat chewing grass (or house plants) may be trying to self-medicate" (Engel, 2002, p. 217).

Note: The author in (b) has changed the upper-case (capital) *A* of the original to lower-case *a*, using the square bracket convention to indicate this change. This is necessary since the quote is no longer an independent sentence but embedded in a sentence following *that*. It is allowed to change the grammar or punctuation of quoted material, indicating the changes by putting square brackets around them, as long as the meaning of the original is preserved.

Now, use the End-Text Citations you produced for the last task (Task 3) and the same source information to help you select the correct In-Text Citation information to place in the citation parentheses below.

Source A

Quotation from page 3 of the script of a play entitled *Pygmalion*, written by George Bernard Shaw, as it appears in the version published in 2000 by Penguin Books of London, UK.

[A] A little over a century ago, George Bernard Shaw made the following claim: "The English have no respect for their language and will not teach their children how to speak it" (____).

[B] It has been famously observed that "[t]he English have no respect for their language and will not teach their children how to speak it"
(_______________________________________).

Source B

Quotation from page 1 of the second edition of a book entitled *A Practical Introduction to Phonetics*, written by John C. Catford and published in 2001 by Oxford University Press of Oxford, UK.

[A] According to Catford, "Any person who works with language would do well to have a basic knowledge of phonetics"
(_______________________________________).

[B] It has been argued that all language professionals should have "a basic knowledge of phonetics" (____).

Source C

Information from a book chapter entitled "Sociolinguistics in the British Isles," written by Jane Stuart-Smith and Bill Haddican. The chapter occupies pages 296–309 of a book entitled *The Routledge Handbook of Sociolinguistics around the World* edited by Martin J. Ball and published in 2010 by Routledge in New York.

[A]   Stuart-Smith and Haddican report that the accent of people from Glasgow, known as Glaswegian, has generally attracted negative judgments in attitude surveys (________________________________).

[B]   The accent of people from Glasgow, known as Glaswegian, has generally attracted negative judgments in attitude surveys
(________________________________).

Source D

Paraphrase of information from an anonymous article entitled "David and Victoria Beckham 'getting posher', study finds" appearing on the BBC News website, dated 17 April 2013, at this URL: http://www.bbc.co.uk/news/uk-england-22179969.

[A]   BBC News recently reported that David Beckham changed his accent after moving to the United States to play for Los Angeles Galaxy
(________________________________).

[B]   Occasionally, individuals adapt their accent to accommodate different audiences, as when the soccer player David Beckham moved to the United States to play for Los Angeles Galaxy
(________________________________).

Source E

Information from an article entitled "Two thousand million?" written by David Crystal, appearing on pages 3–6 of Volume 24, Issue 1, of the journal entitled *English Today* published in March 2008.

[A]   Crystal estimates that a third of the world's population today speak English
(________________________________).

[B]   It is believed by some linguists that today a third of the world's population speak English (________________________________).

Note: Some books and articles you read may have a section called a **Bibliography**. A Bibliography is different from End-Text Citations and may include sources not cited but which the writer is suggesting that the reader might like to read.

Warning

In the End-Text Citations in the APA system, you must *not* include any works which you have not cited in the text. When you are finalizing your paper, check that:

☐ Every In-Text Citation has a matching entry in your End-Text Citations;

☐ Every entry in your End-Text Citations has a matching In-Text Citation.

Tip

Print off your End-Text Citations and read through the paper, making sure you can check the above boxes.

How To

Document Sources

Make sure that your research paper contains the following elements:

- A single system of documentation which you apply consistently throughout;
- **In-Text Citations** for every use of sources;
- An **End-Text** list of **Citations** for every source.

WHAT GOES ON INSIDE THE WRITER'S HEAD

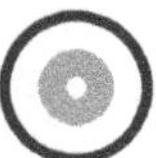

UNIT FOCUS

In this Unit, you will be able to see:

- How a writer goes about the task of researching and writing up an article;

- How important summarizing is in almost all writing activities;

- How a writer presents two or more summaries to produce the kind of balance which you will need to produce in your papers;

- How writers "orchestrate" the content in different ways to achieve different purposes.

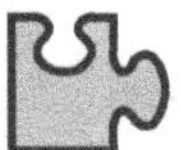

CONTEXT

Journalistic Brief

Try to put yourself in the position of a journalist who is assigned the following brief:

- To write a Report on a recent measure banning bottle-feeding for babies;
- To include in the Report the arguments in defense of bottle-feeding.

Try to organize the Report article in your head in such a way as to get across the overall point that banning bottle-feeding is a *bad* idea.

Working Notes

Obviously, you can't know for sure what goes through anyone's head before starting on a writing task or assignment, but you should by now be able to make informed guesses.

Before writing the article you are about to read in this Unit, the journalist would most likely have made a "to-do" list something like this:

To-Do List

☐ Summarize and synthesize the various points made in the case for promoting breastfeeding and banning bottle-feeding.

☐ Acknowledge the strength of the case for breastfeeding and at the same time mention that there are problems with this case.

☐ Summarize and synthesize at some length the various points made in the case for allowing bottle-feeding.

☐ Conclude with a statement indicating the strength of the case summarized last (i.e. allowing bottle-feeding).

☐ Put together the two summaries in such a way as to give more weight and credibility to the case for allowing bottle-feeding (e.g. by presenting the breastfeeding arguments first and the bottle-feeding arguments last).

Schematically, we can represent the first four points of the list in actual words, as follows:

Synthesis 1: Baby bottles ought to be banned for various reasons.

Bridge: Such proposals are clearly well-meaning, and bottle-feeding does have problems.

Synthesis 2: Passing laws that place restrictions on women's parenting choices is not the solution.

Conclusion: In the end, laws like this end up hurting the very women and children they claim to protect.

WORDS IN CONTEXT

Using a dictionary if necessary, make sure you understand each word in bold and check the box before moving to the next item.

In an effort to **promote** (*encourage*) breastfeeding	☐
legislators (*lawmakers*)	☐
considering a proposal (*discussing a possible new law*) to ban baby bottles	☐
The **legislation** (*law*) also **makes sense** (*is a good idea*)	☐
laws like this **end up** (*unintentionally cause*) hurting	☐
shoot this proposal **down** (*stop it becoming a law*)	☐
lowers a child's risk of developing obesity (*makes children less likely to become obese*)	☐
well-meaning (*with good intentions*)	☐
transnational companies (*big companies operating in many countries*)	☐
formula (*powder you add water to*)	☐
Nestlé **pushed** (*advertised*) formula feeding **aggressively** (*strongly*)	☐
to **stop by** (*visit*) women's houses	☐
in light of (*taking account of*) this history	☐
to breastfeed **every few hours** (*at intervals of a few hours*)	☐
may have trouble **latching on** (*finding the mother's nipple and sucking successfully*)	☐
while **juggling** (*balancing and meeting the demands of*) a home and a career	☐
adults **raised on** (*who grew up drinking*) formula	☐
can **attest** (*give proof of*)	☐
by no means (*certainly not*) a death sentence	☐
another **downside to** (*disadvantage of*) this proposal	☐

THE TEXT

Let's now take a look at how the journalist actually implemented the various steps in the to-do list in the process of writing.

☑ Summarize and synthesize the various points made in the case for promoting breastfeeding and banning bottle-feeding

> In an effort to promote breastfeeding, Venezuela's Congress is considering a proposal to ban baby bottles entirely within the country. Odalis Monzon, one of the legislators behind the measure, spoke on state television last Thursday, saying "We want to increase the love (between mother and child) because this has been lost as a result of these transnational companies selling formula."
>
> …
>
> The proposed legislation is clearly well-meaning. Scientists and doctors have known for years that breastfeeding has a number of benefits for infants. It protects against common childhood illnesses, lowers a child's risk of developing obesity and diabetes later in life, and best of all…unlike formula, it's 100% free.
>
> The legislation also makes sense when you look at how formula has been marketed worldwide. For decades, companies like Nestlé pushed formula feeding aggressively in developing nations, giving away free samples in maternity wards and sometimes even hiring sales girls in nurse uniforms to stop by women's houses.

☑ Acknowledge the strength of the case for breastfeeding and at the same time mention that there are problems with this case

> It's easy to understand why Venezuela would want to promote breastfeeding in light of this history with formula companies, but passing laws that place restrictions on women's parenting choices is not the solution.
>
> The truth is, formula may not be quite as healthy as breast milk, but…

☑ Summarize and synthesize at some length the various points made in the case for allowing bottlefeeding

> …not all mothers are able to breastfeed. Some mothers may have infectious diseases or be taking medications that prevent them from breastfeeding. Some babies may have trouble latching on. Some women may simply find breastfeeding painful or uncomfortable – or they may not have the time while juggling a home and a career. As millions of adults raised on formula can attest, it is by no means a death sentence.
>
> …
>
> There's also another downside to this proposal – it penalizes working moms who want to pump breast milk for their children. Very few workplaces would allow a woman to bring her child to the office for the first six months or year of life to breastfeed every few hours. (And employers are already likely to look down on breastfeeding employees anyway.) Without bottles, how is a woman supposed to store pumped milk for her child?

☑ Conclude with a statement indicating the strength of the case summarized last (allowing bottle-feeding)

> In the end, laws like this end up hurting the very women and children they claim to protect. Hopefully, Venezuela will do the right thing and shoot this proposal down this week.
>
> Rodriguez, J. M. (2013, June 18). Bottle-feeding bans are harmful for moms and babies. Care2 website. http://www.care2.com/causes/bottle-feeding-bans-are-harmful-for-moms-and-babies.html#ixzz2XE9UsFJn.

Notice how the writer has also managed to:

☑ Orchestrate the two syntheses in such a way as to give more weight and credibility to the case for allowing bottlefeeding, for example, by presenting the breastfeeding arguments first and the bottle-feeding arguments last.

GRAMMAR IN CONTEXT

1. Determiners

Because the breastfeeding text is about a ban, which would effectively mean "*No* mothers would be allowed to bottle-feed their children" and "*All* mothers would have to breastfeed," whether or not the law would be appropriate for *all* mothers in *all* situations is very important to the author. Notice the words in bold in the sentences below which focus on this point.

General	Specific	Differences between general and specific
…**not all** mothers are able to breastfeed.	…**not all** <u>of the</u> mothers in this hospital are able to breastfeed.	
Some mothers may have infectious diseases…	**Some** <u>of those</u> mothers may have infectious diseases…	Unlike the general examples (column 1) the specific examples (column 2) all have the word *of* + a determiner (underlined) before the noun. They may also have additional specifying information.
Some babies may have trouble latching on.	**Some** <u>of these</u> babies may have trouble latching on.	
Some women may simply find breastfeeding painful or uncomfortable…	**Some** <u>of her</u> women patients may simply find breastfeeding painful or uncomfortable…	
Very few workplaces would allow a woman to bring her child to the office…	**Very few** <u>of the</u> workplaces in that area had special rooms for nursing mothers.	

The words in bold in the first column (sometimes called *quantifiers*) are used for talking about numbers of people or things in **general**. The same words in the second column, when followed by *of* + words like *the, these, those, my,* etc. (sometimes called *determiners*), are used for talking about **specific** people or things.

Note also from the examples below that *few* and *a few,* whether or not they are followed by *of*, are *quite different* in meaning.

General	Specific	Notes on meaning
A few people paid attention.	**A few** of Jane's friends came.	• not all (similar to some)
We had **a few** laughs on that trip.	**A few** of my investments paid off.	• as many as you would expect
Few people paid attention.	**Few** of Jane's friends came.	• not very many
We had **few** laughs on that trip.	**Few** of my investments paid off.	• not as many as you would expect

☑ TASK

Choose the most appropriate of the expressions in brackets (quantifier or quantifier + *of* + determiner) for each of the following contexts. We have done the first example for you.

1. Since 1934, [**all** / **all of the**] UK citizens wishing to drive a motor vehicle have been required to pass a driving proficiency test.

2. Not serving meat dishes in India is unreasonable: **[not all / not all of the]** Indians are vegetarians.

3. Serving only meat dishes at this party is unreasonable: **[some / some of the]** guests are vegetarians.

4. **[Some / some of the]** people prefer not to eat any dairy products.

5. By September, **[most / most of the]** US citizens living in Dubai had registered at the consulate.

6. **[Most / most of the]** US citizens possess a driver's license.

7. **[Few / few of the]** students in that college are clever enough to take 12 courses.

8. **[Very few / Very few of the]** people remember the great flu pandemic of 1919.

9. Although most children are vaccinated against tuberculosis at school, **[few / a few]** individuals always slip through the net.

10. Because most children are vaccinated against tuberculosis at school, **[few/ a few]** people alive today will ever contract the disease.

11. In Statistics 101, **[few of / a few of]** my classmates are very clever: they always get 100% in quizzes.

12. In Statistics 101, **[few of / a few of]** my classmates are very clever: no one ever gets 100%.

2. Revision

For convenience, we have assembled below the various components of the bottle-feeding text (some omissions of text – ellipsis – are shown by three dots).

In an effort to promote breastfeeding, Venezuela's Congress is considering a proposal to ban baby bottles entirely within the country. Odalis Monzon, one of the legislators behind the measure, spoke on state television last Thursday, saying "We want to increase the love (between mother and child) because this has been lost as a result of these transnational companies selling formula."

…

The proposed legislation is clearly well-meaning. Scientists and doctors have known for years that breastfeeding has a number of benefits for infants. It protects against common childhood illnesses, lowers a child's risk of developing obesity and diabetes later in life, and best of all…unlike formula, it's 100% free.

The legislation also makes sense when you look at how formula has been marketed worldwide. For decades, companies like Nestlé pushed formula feeding aggressively in developing nations, giving away free samples in maternity wards and sometimes even hiring sales girls in nurse uniforms to stop by women's houses.

It's easy to understand why Venezuela would want to promote breastfeeding in light of this history with formula companies, but passing laws that place restrictions on women's parenting choices is not the solution.

The truth is, formula may not be quite as healthy as breast milk, but…

… not all mothers are able to breastfeed. Some mothers may have infectious diseases or be taking medications that prevent them from breastfeeding. Some babies may have trouble latching on. Some women may simply find breastfeeding painful or uncomfortable – or they may not have the time while juggling a home and a career. As millions of adults raised on formula can attest, it is by no means a death sentence.

…

There's also another downside to this proposal – it penalizes working moms who want to pump breast milk for their children. Very few workplaces would allow a woman to bring her child to the office for the first six months or year of life to breastfeed every few hours. (And employers are already likely to look down on breastfeeding employees anyway.) Without bottles, how is a woman supposed to store pumped milk for her child?

In the end, laws like this end up hurting the very women and children they claim to protect. Hopefully, Venezuela will do the right thing and shoot this proposal down this week.

Fill in the spaces below by finding in the text at least *one example* of each of the grammatical features we list, which have been described in earlier units. We have filled in some examples for you.

Unit	Feature	Example
A	Modal verbs	
A	Hedging expressions	
B	Present Perfect Tense	
C	*–ing* forms: Gerunds	to promote breastfeeding
C	*–ing* forms: Participles	
C	Noun + Noun compounds	baby bottles
D	Passive verbs	
D	Reports in the Simple Present	
D	Reports in the Simple Past	
E	Noun + *to* Infinitive	an effort to promote
E	Adjective + *to* Infinitive	
E	Verb + *to* Infinitive	
E	*This* to refer to previous text	
F	Real Conditional Sentences	
F	Ellipsis	
G	*That* to report propositions	

 # TEXT ORGANIZATION

☑ TASK 1

Think about the following questions:

In this article, which is the Given information?

a. Breastfeeding is superior to bottle-feeding?

b. Bottle-feeding is superior to breastfeeding?

Now think about the title of the newspaper article:

"Bottle-feeding Bans Are Harmful for Moms and Babies"

Would you say the title of the article is

a. Effective since it captures the Given and the New in a particularly subtle way?

b. Ineffective because it reveals the writer's intention too explicitly?

If you agree that (b) the title is ineffective because it is too explicit, can you suggest a more subtle or more effective title?

Title [revised]

- -

☑ TASK 2

In this article, there is no Lead Summary, which would ideally capture the Given (*breastfeeding is good*) and the New (*breastfeeding has problems*), using highly vivid, attention-grabbing language. See if you can write this kind of Lead Summary.

Lead Summary [added]

- -

- -

☑ TASK 3

In this article there is no Overview. You may remember from Unit B that ideally an Overview:

- Gets attention
- Sets the scene
- States the Given
- States the New
- Offers a map of the article

Write an overview that carries out these functions:

Overview [added]

☑ TASK 4

In the existing article, what we are calling **Synthesis 1** starts rather abruptly:

> In an effort to promote breastfeeding, Venezuela's Congress is considering a proposal to ban baby bottles entirely within the country…

From Unit E on Explanatory Synthesis you may recall that ideally such a synthesis opens with an introduction that sets the scene. It does so to introduce the common topic of the various studies or the positions summarized. Such a scene-setting introduction may include

- a quote
- an anecdote
- a general statement

Can you draft such a global scene-setter to precede Synthesis 1 (reasons for promoting breastfeeding and banning bottle-feeding)?

Synthesis 1: Introduction [added]

ASSIGNMENT

If you now put the various elements you produced together with the existing elements we set out and illustrated earlier, you will end up with the following overall structure:

Title

Lead Summary

Overview

Synthesis 1 (now including an introduction)

Bridge

Synthesis 2

Conclusion

Now, try to rewrite the article in about 500–600 words using

1. the added material you developed above;

2. extra material researched by you to summarize in both Synthesis 1 and Synthesis 2.

For the extra material you will need for item 2, you can use online resources to find more detailed information on the various arguments for and against breastfeeding and bottle-feeding.

Here are some online sites which you might find helpful. Some of them were hyperlinked in the original article.

Synthesis 1 (Arguments for Breastfeeding): Sources

Shoichet, C. E. (2013, June 18). Breast-feeding is best, so ban bottles, Venezuelan lawmaker proposes. *CNN*.
http://edition.cnn.com/2013/06/17/health/venezuela-baby-bottle-ban/index.html

Parrasch, S. (2013, February 18). 830,000 Reasons Why Breast Is Best. Care2 website.
http://www.care2.com/causes/830000-reasons-why-breast-is-best.
html#ixzz2XE0P10sT

Molland, J. (2010, December 20). Can Breastfeeding Prevent Childhood Obesity? Care2 website.
http://www.care2.com/causes/can-breastfeeding-prevent-childhood-obesity.
html#ixzz2XDuUWpc2

Synthesis 2 (Arguments for Bottle-feeding): Sources

Celizic, M. (2009, March 16). Is breast-feeding really best? Today website. http://www.today.com/id/29718562/ns/today-parenting_and_family/t/breast-feeding-really-best/%23.UcBT6_ZgZTM#.Ucl1lzs3Bip

Thomson-DeVeaux, A. (2011, March 24). Breastfeeding Women Perceived As Less Competent. Care2 website. http://www.care2.com/causes/breastfeeding-women-perceived-as-less-competent.html#ixzz2XDy2XYAZ

Ingall, M. (2006, December 11). The Breastfeeding Myth. Babble website. http://www.babble.com/baby/breastfeeding-vs-bottle-feeding-why-baby-formula-is-not-so-bad/

Note: Many of these websites have links to other sources you may find helpful also.

WHAT GOES ON INSIDE THE BEGINNER WRITER'S HEAD

 ## UNIT FOCUS

In this Unit, you will be able to see:

- How a beginner writer goes about the task of researching and writing up a research paper;

- How such a writer might go about seeking and using help from others in editing a paper;

- How editors can use the models of good writing demonstrated in this book.

 ## CONTEXT

Obviously, we can't know what goes on inside a beginner writer's head; but by looking at what the person writes, we can make an attempt to recreate the process. In this Unit, we will look at:

1. An outline of the first draft of a research paper by a beginner writer

2. An outline of a second draft of the same paper after consultation with a more experienced writer

3. Suggestions for improving the second draft, using the principles presented and modeled in this book

4. A final improved draft

The topic which the student chose to research and write about was "The Ethics of Animal Experimentation" (a debate between supporters and opponents which you will recall was partly covered in the text for Unit G).

Having done some preliminary research, the student opted for the following Thesis:

> Animal Experimentation is ethically justifiable.

First Draft Outline

An outline of the student's essay would look like this:

Title

Introduction

Synthesis 1: Case for Animal Experimentation

[1] **Argument (Moral/Social)**   It is unethical to use humans for testing.

[2] **Argument (Medical)**   It is useful for trialing techniques and tools.

[3] **Argument (Medical)**   There are no viable alternatives.

Synthesis 2: Case against Animal Experimentation

[1] **Argument (Moral/Social)**   Animals suffer pain.

Conclusion

Discussion Point

What problems can you see with the organization of this outline?

Commentary

The outline of the first draft is rather unbalanced: there are three points in favor of animal experimentation and only one against. There is also an ordering problem: before presenting a case *for* a particular position, it is better to present the arguments *against* that position first.

Second Draft Outline

The student showed this draft to a more experienced writer, and in response the student wrote a second draft. An outline of this second draft looked like this:

Title

Overview

Synthesis 1: Arguments for Animal Experimentation

[1] **Argument (Moral/Social)**   It is unethical to use humans for testing.

[2] **Argument (Medical)**   It is useful for trialing techniques and tools.

[3] **Argument (Medical)**   There are no viable alternatives.

Synthesis 2: Arguments against Animal Experimentation

[1] **Argument (Moral/Social)**   Animals suffer pain.

[2] **Argument (Medical)**   That serious illnesses cannot be cured shows it is futile.

[3] **Argument (Medical)**   Animals and humans differ.

[4] **Argument (Medical)**   There are viable alternatives.

Conclusion

Discussion Point

Can you see any further problems with this expanded outline?

Commentary

Ideally, research papers present clearly a Given assumption and a New correction of that assumption. The writer would present the Given-New contrast clearly both in the opening (Title, Lead Summary, and Overview) and in the overall ordering of the paper (i.e. which position is presented first).

As the student wants this paper to argue *in favor of* Animal Experimentation, s/he could, for example:

- deal with the arguments against Animal Experimentation as a New problem;
- move on to presenting the New arguments for animal experimentation.

The thrust of the paper would then be the New correction, namely that, despite all of its problems, Animal Experimentation *is* justifiable.

Extracts from the Second Draft Examined

Let's now look in more detail at various components of the student's second draft. Below for each component we present general *criteria*, the student's actual *text*, and our *commentary* on how well the student has met the criteria.

Title

Criteria

Titles should

☐ be attention-grabbing; and

☐ contain both Given and New positions.

Student's text

Can Animal Experimentation be justified?

Commentary

☑ Title is attention-grabbing; but note inconsistent use of upper case.

☑ Title contains both Given and New positions. The title also subtly promotes the New.

Lead Summary

Criteria

A lead summary should

☐ be a short (20–30 words), attention-grabbing, descriptive summary of what the paper is going to be about; and

☐ capture the Given and New of the paper using vivid language.

Student's text

[No lead summary]

Commentary

We recommend adding a lead summary.

Overview

Criteria

An overview (a paragraph or two) should:

☐ grab the attention with something like an anecdote, a quotation, or a question;

- ☐ capture the Given and the New in the form of a general statement;

- ☐ make some kind of emotional connection with the reader, by approaching the issue in a personal and not too formal manner; and

- ☐ provide a map of the rest of the paper: how the paper is structured, including the order in which the various issues will be covered.

Student's text

> *"Ask the experimenters why they experiment on animals and the answer is: 'Because animals are like us.' Ask the experimenters why it is morally okay to experiment on animals, and the answer is: 'Because the animals are not like us.' Animal experimentation rests on a logical contradiction."* **(Charles R. Magel, as cited in Taylor, 2011, p.76)**

Animal experimentation is the use of animals in research and development projects. It has caused a constant debate. Some people, especially scientists, researchers, and patients, support it, while some believe that it expresses the cruelty and inhumanity of scientists and researchers. Each group has its own reasons to support or to reject animal experimentation.

Commentary

☑ The opening quotation grabs attention and makes the reader think.

☑ This opening paradox captures the Given and New contrast. Confusingly, however, it concludes by favoring a position which the paper will not actually adopt. A Given and New contrast is presented fairly clearly in terms of a constant debate.

☒ However, the language is somewhat formal and impersonal.

☑ The paper follows a kind of map in that both the quotation and the other paragraph follow the same order:
    (a) support
    (b) reject

☒ However, this map is inadequate in three ways:
1. As the writer intends to favor the support position, he or she should present it last:
    (a) reject
    (b) support
2. The map should be more explicit.
3. The writer does not give enough detail about the order of arguments adopted within the presentation of each position, specifically, that he/she will address social/moral issues before the medical issues. (Look at the second draft outline above.)

Synthesis 1

Criteria

The first body section of an effective paper should contain

☐ a synthesis of views (drawn from one or more studies) expressing the *Given* position.

☐ a global introduction which sets the scene for the various positions to be summarized.

Student's text A

Scientists believe that the use of animals in experiments is important and should be accepted by the society because it helps in creating medicines and insuring their safety, it contributes greatly in developing surgical techniques and medical tools, and it has no effective replacement. And they mentioned many reasons to get the support from the society.

Commentary

☒ As we already noted, the student has probably confused the reader by choosing to present the New position first rather than the Given.

☒ The first sentence of the global introduction to this synthesis presents an accurate map of the medical arguments for animal experimentation.

☒ The last sentence confusingly introduces social arguments. This creates uncertainty: what will the paper actually deal with first?

Student's text B

Animal experimentation is justified by good reasons on the social level and on the medical level. On the social level, scientists believe that people should be treated respectfully and with mercy…

Commentary

☒ The opening sentence here rather unnecessarily restates that there are social and medical arguments before clarifying that the paper will actually deal with social arguments first.

Student's text C

On the medical level, these experiments help a great deal in finding the correct medicines in many aspects. First, the use of animal experimentation helps create new medicines that are safe to use…

Commentary

☑ This paragraph usefully tells the reader the paper is now shifting to the medical arguments, and then helpfully signals the first of these arguments – the valuable role of animal experimentation in creating new medicines.

Bridge

Criteria

As we indicated in Unit I, where a definite conclusion to Synthesis 1 is absent, it is helpful for the writer to provide a bridging connection between Synthesis 1 and Synthesis 2. A bridge should

☐ explicitly prepare the reader for the shift from Given to New.

Student's text

However, many people reject animal experimentation and find it unethical and unacceptable. They present reasons logical enough to persuade people to stop this kind of experiment.

Commentary

☒ Here the word *However* is not weighty enough to serve as a bridge. This paragraph is not a bridge but in fact the beginning of Synthesis 2.

Synthesis 2

Criteria

The second main part of an effective paper should contain

☐ a synthesis of views (drawn from one or more studies) arguing the case for the New.

Student's text

However, many people reject animal experimentation and find it unethical and unacceptable. They present reasons logical enough to persuade people to stop these kinds of experiments. If people cannot bear pain and torture, why do they believe it is normal to torture animals? Do they think that animals do not feel pain? Do they not claim that animals share many qualities with humans? Animals feel pain and cry silently.… One more ethical reason: a great number of animals die every year in laboratories because of chemicals tested by the pharmaceutical industry. According to Dr Bernhard Rambeck, who rejects animal experimentation, playing down of the suffering of lab animals is an evil claim because they have been bred, kept, and transported under artificial conditions.…

Commentary

The global introduction to the synthesis is weak.

☒ Unlike the introduction to Synthesis 1, it does not map out the various arguments it will then go on to summarize.

☒ The various arguments are not clearly signaled. Unlike in Synthesis 1, they are not arranged into paragraphs.

☒ Given the writer's support for animal experimentation, evaluating the anti-animal experimentation case as logical enough to persuade does not make sense. It seems that the writer apparently now endorses two contradictory opinions.

☒ The writer does not attribute the first two arguments summarized, so it seems as if the writer is making the argument.

Conclusion

Criteria

Ideally a Conclusion should contain

☐ a brief re-statement of the Given

☐ a brief re-statement of the New

☐ a punchline, a finale, a dramatic close

Student's text

To conclude, animals have been used in experiments in medicine industries and research. Although scientists and researchers justify this process, many people are strongly against it, mainly for moral reasons. Researchers are trying to find a suitable and an effective substitute, but still no new alternatives have been found.

Commentary

☒ Here, as throughout the paper, the writer confuses the reader by presenting New before Given.

☒ The re-statement of the New could be improved by reminding us of the main bases of the case for animal experimentation, rather than merely telling us that there is a case.

☒ The re-statement of the Given is fuller but still too vague. The final sentence is not dramatic enough. By emphasizing the lack of alternatives rather than the ethical consequences of this lack, it fails to address explicitly enough the ethical question the paper began by asking – *Can Animal Experimentation be justified*?

☑ TASK A

Look again at the student's title and see if you can think of one or more other effective titles, keeping the above Given and New in mind.

☑ TASK B

Based on the content of the paper you have seen above, can you write a Lead Summary for this paper?

☑ TASK C

Try to write a better Overview for the paper. See if you can include a better and more detailed map which would show that the paper will deal, in the following order, with the arguments against Animal Experimentation and the arguments for Animal Experimentation, and that, within each, there will be a medical/scientific and a social/moral side.

☑ TASK D

Now see if you can provide a new Synthesis 1, this time arguing for the Given, with a proper global scene-setter and summarizing one study.

☑ TASK E

Follow this by providing a Bridge between Synthesis 1 and Synthesis 2.

☑ TASK F

Now you can go on to provide a new Synthesis 2, but this time arguing for the New, with a proper global scene-setter and summarizing one study.

☑ TASK G

Finally, see if you can provide a Conclusion for the paper.

SUGGESTED VERSION

On the next few pages, you can read a revised version of the student's second draft, taking account of the points raised in the commentary sections on that draft. After that there is an annotated version of the same text.

The formatting of the paper and its citation style is APA.

An outline of the paper would look something like this:

Title

Lead Summary

Overview

Synthesis 1: Arguments against Animal Experimentation

[1]	**Argument (Ethical)**	Humans do not have the right to cause animals pain.
[2]	**Argument (Medical)**	Animals and humans differ, so the results are useless.
[3]	**Argument (Medical)**	There are viable alternatives.
	Conclusion	Summary of case.

Bridge

Synthesis 2: Arguments for Animal Experimentation

[1]	**Argument (Ethical)**	Humans have the right to use animals for testing.
[2]	**Argument (Medical)**	It is useful for trialing techniques and tools.
[3]	**Argument (Medical)**	It can be reduced but not replaced entirely by alternatives.
	Conclusion	Summary of case.

Conclusion

Can Animal Experimentation Be Justified?

Terry Smith
Utopia University

Can Animal Experimentation Be Justified?

The hotly debated question of whether humans should continue to carry out medical experiments on animals involves complex issues of both a practical and an ethical kind.

Ask the experimenters why they experiment on animals and the answer is: "Because animals are like us." Ask the experimenters why it is morally okay to experiment on animals, and the answer is: "Because the animals are not like us." (Taylor, 2011, p. 76)

The monkey's sad, scared eyes stare out at me. Its hands grip the bars of its cage. Tubes and wires from lab equipment are taped to its partly shaved skull. I came across this haunting image on the internet recently, on an animal rights site. My first instinct is to try to forget the image and think of something else. But is that responsible? As a citizen, I not only allow animals to be treated like this, but am likely to be paying for it through taxes or medical charities. In this paper, rather than avoid the uncomfortable issue being raised by animal rights campaigners, I will attempt to confront it: Is the use of animals for medical research justifiable?

In attempting to answer this question, the essay will consider the various arguments for and against animal experimentation in medical research as made by animal rights campaigners and medical researchers. These in turn draw on the views of scientists, philosophers, and the major world religions. I will begin by reporting the arguments against animal experimentation. In discussing both the cases against and for, I will deal with the ethical and social aspects of the case before moving to the technical ones.

The ethical case against animal experimentation is based on the position that animals, particularly more intelligent animals, are similar to humans. Importantly, animals are like humans in having the capacity to feel pain. Animal experimentation requires animals to feel pain: "Animal experiments in the area of toxicology, cancer research, surgery and radiation research, amongst others, are not conceivable without considerable suffering"; in toxicology experiments, for example, "the animal is poisoned, sometimes more sometimes less quickly" (Rambeck, n.d.). As humans, we only inflict pain on other humans with their consent and for some agreed benefit. For example, doctors carry out painful operations or administer painful chemotherapy to patients in order to help them stay alive or live in less pain than before. Animal rights proponents argue that animals which are used in medical experiments, by contrast, can in no way benefit from the pain they suffer – and it is therefore unethical to inflict pain upon them. According to this view, humans who support animal experimentation are guilty of what some philosophers have described as "speciesism." Speciesism has been defined as "[b]y analogy with racism and sexism, the improper stance of refusing respect to the lives, dignity, or needs of animals of other than the human species" (Blackburn, 2005).

A technical argument made by the opponents of animal experimentation is that it is actually unhelpful. An article in the British Medical Journal, for example, reviewed several studies involving animal research and argued that there was "little evidence" to support the common assumption "that animal research has contributed to the treatment of human disease" (Pound, Ebrahim, Sandercock, Brack, & Roberts, 2004, p. 514). The same study concluded that "Even if animal experiments provide valid results and sufficiently precise estimates of treatment effects to discount the effects of chance, the extent to which the results can reasonably be generalized to humans remains open to question" (Pound et al., 2004, p. 517). This surprising conclusion may be based on the view that differences in the "anatomy, physiology and metabolism" of humans and animals make it impossible "to predict whether a human will react identically or differently based on the results of experiments conducted on animals" (Gericke, n.d.). For example, a 1983 study of carcinogenic substances conducted by the pharmaceutical company Pfizer found that "only 5–25% of the substances harmful to humans" also had adverse effects on experimental animals (Gericke, n.d.).

If it is indeed the case that the results of animal experimentation are effectively useless, this leads naturally to the third argument often made by opponents of animal experimentation. This argument is that the resources currently allocated to animal experimentation should instead be allocated to other medical improvement strategies such as "epidemiology, clinical research, occupational safety and health, and social medicine" (Rambeck, n.d.). A related position is that resources currently being wasted on animal experimentation should be diverted to developing hi-tech alternatives to animal testing, such as the use of human cells and tissues in combination with specialized computer programs (Gernicke, n.d.).

To summarize the case against animal experimentation, then, we can see that in the terms of the parable in the quotation with which this paper opened, opponents of animal experimentation wish to contradict both statements attributed to the experimenters. Let us note in passing that their position is in one sense similar to that of their opponents. They too wish to argue that animals are similar and dissimilar to humans. While they affirm that animals are similar to humans morally, in that both animals and humans feel pain and both have the right to avoid having pain inflicted on them against their will, opponents of animal experimentation deny the medical similarity of animals to humans. They argue instead that there is a physical dissimilarity, which means that animal experimentation is at best both useless and wasteful, and at worst, dangerously misleading.

Let us now consider the case for animal experimentation, again starting with ethics. When the experimenters argue that animals are different from humans, they are implicitly arguing that animals are not only different from humans but inferior, in some sense, to humans. This moral difference means that it is justifiable to cause suffering to animals to alleviate suffering by humans. This position is the one we have seen that animal rights advocates define as speciesism. The evidence of many human practices and institutions, such as livestock-keeping, hunting, and legal systems throughout the world, all suggest that human cultures generally have implicitly regarded human life as more important than animal life. Does such speciesism have any ethical basis? Most of the major world religions do in fact explicitly attribute more importance to human life and well-being than that of other species. Judaism, Christianity, and Islam seem to broadly agree that God has given man a unique status and authority over other beings he has created. In Hinduism and Buddhism humans are also superior to other animals in being nearer to gods in the progress of reincarnation (Waldau, 2001, pp. 23–29). On an everyday level, it seems fair to assume that while they might not argue the case for speciesism, most human beings would demonstrate speciesism in practice. For example, if there was a choice to be made between a possibly dangerous new drug or surgical technique being tried out first on an animal before it was used on their own child, I guess that most parents would consent to the animal test, rather than, say, volunteer themselves or hire another human subject.

This leads to the technical argument of whether animal experimentation is actually useful or not. The US National Research Council points to various examples of how animal experimentation has in fact been useful. For example, the development of successful vaccines against many diseases which caused thousands of deaths in childhood at the turn of the last century – smallpox, polio, diphtheria, whooping cough – has caused them to be almost completely eradicated (National Research Council, 2004, p. 9). These vaccines all needed development and testing using animal models, as is still happening now in the development of anti-malarial vaccines. In the field of surgery, the Council also points out that heart valve replacement, organ transplants, and coronary artery bypasses are now common procedures which "would not have been possible without animal research": specifically, "the technique of sewing blood vessels together was developed through surgeries on dogs and cats" (National Research Council, 2004, p. 17). Interestingly, in light of the debate around human "speciesism," it is also pointed out by supporters that animals themselves too have benefited and will benefit from animal experimentation: for example, dogs have benefited from veterinary doctors' use of "medicines for diabetes, pacemakers for heart irregularities, hip and joint replacements for degenerative conditions, chemotherapy for cancer and vaccines against rabies" (Paul, 2002, p. 10).

Lastly, there is the issue of alternatives to animal experimentation. Supporters of animal experimentation "acknowledge the need for alternatives to reduce animal suffering" using criteria "often described as the three Rs of biomedical research…Reduction, Replacement, Refinement" (Murnaghan, 2010). Laws regulating the use of animals mean that ethical review panels require researchers to apply these criteria (Paul, 2002, p. 14). Refinement may involve, for example, using less invasive techniques than surgery, such as MRI scanning; such techniques may also mean there is Reduction, namely, fewer animals need to be used ("Mice, MRI's and Microchips," 2012). Suffering may also be reduced by humane attention to the animals' welfare involving both anesthesia and euthanasia where appropriate. However, Replacement is difficult to achieve because, it is argued, "animals are often the best and sometimes the only way to test the effect of medicines or other chemicals"; this is because of the difficulty of replicating the way animals "contain organs connected together in an incredibly complex system, just like humans" ("Mice, MRI's and Microchips" 2012).

To conclude this discussion of the position of animal experimentation proponents, we shall return to the parable in the opening quotation of this paper. We can now see that this position seems to be a mirror image of their opponents' position, and also draws attention to both similarity and dissimilarity. According to this position, while animals are not the same as humans, they are the most similar thing there is to us, and therefore the most safe thing on which we can possibly test new treatments and drugs. On the other hand, animals are dissimilar from humans on some moral level. If animals were not, in this moral sense, less important than humans, it would indeed be wrong to cause them to suffer on our behalf. However, there seems to be a fundamental assumption among supporters of animal experimentation that in the final analysis human life is more important than the lives of other animals. As we have seen, some animal rights supporters label supporters of animal experimentation as speciesists who refuse to respect animals' interests. I would argue that the term speciesism is itself both an ad hominem attack and an either/or fallacy: in practice, it does seem possible for humans to place animals' interests below those of humans, while at the same time respecting animals' interests, for example, by implementing ethical guidelines for animal testing such as the 3 Rs.

In conclusion, to answer the research question of this paper, Is Animal Experimentation Justifiable, there seem to be two issues involved. One is whether or not animal experimentation is useful: Are animals similar enough to humans for it to be worthwhile experimenting on them? If they are not, it seems clear that animal experimentation cannot be justified. Overall, on the basis of the evidence discussed here, despite limitations on similarity, I believe the objective case for similarity has been made more convincingly than the case against. Animals appear to be similar enough to humans to mean that animal experimentation can be helpful in advancing human healthcare. The second issue is whether or not animal experimentation is ethical: Are animals similar enough to humans for it to be immoral to experiment on them? Or, are humans, in some essential way, superior to animals and therefore entitled to cause animals suffering in order to reduce human suffering? Any response to this second question must be subjective in that it will depend on the worldview of the individual asked. Worldviews differ on the rights and responsibilities which belong to god(s), humans, and animals. According to the worldview of this writer, haunted as I am by the thought of animals suffering, human life does take priority over animal life, and animal experimentation can, therefore, be justified.

References

Blackburn, S. (2005). Speciesism. *The Oxford dictionary of philosophy* (p. 346). Oxford: Oxford University Press.

Gericke, C. (n.d.) Why animal experiments are not necessary. Retrieved from Doctors Against Animal Experiments Germany website: http://aerzte-gegen-tierversuche.de/en/component/content/article/55-resources/244-why-animal-experiments-are-not-necessary

Mice, MRI's and microchips. (2012, December 11). Retrieved from Understanding Animal Research website: http://www.understandinganimalresearch.org.uk/news/2012/12/mice-mri-and-microchips/

Murnaghan, I. (2010, October 12). Refining the alternatives to animal testing. Retrieved from About Animal Testing website: http://www.aboutanimaltesting.co.uk/refining-alternatives-animal-testing.html

Paul, E. F. (2002). Why animal experimentation matters. *Society*, *39*(6), 7–15.

Pound, P., Ebrahim, S., Sandercock, P., Bracken, M. B., & Roberts, I. (2004). Where is the evidence that animal research benefits humans? *British Medical Journal*, *328*: 514–517.

Rambeck, B. (n.d.) The myths of animal experiments. Retrieved from Doctors Against Animal Experiments Germany website: http://www.aerzte-gegen-tierversuche.de/en/resources/general/183-the-myths-of-animal-experiments

Taylor, E. (2011). *What if? The challenge of self-realization*. Carlsbad, CA: Hay House.

The National Research Council. (2004). *Science, medicine, and animals* Washington, DC: The National Academies Press.

Waldau, P. (2001). *The specter of speciesism: Buddhist and Christian views of animals*. Oxford: Oxford University Press.

REVISED VERSION WITH COMMENTS

Below is an annotated version of the revised paper. We have commented in the right-hand margin on the specific functions of different parts of the paper and the purpose of the revisions.

Can Animal Experimentation Be Justified?

The hotly debated question of whether humans should continue to carry out medical experiments on animals involves complex issues of both a practical and an ethical kind.

A Lead Summary has been added, capturing the Given and New contrast.

Ask the experimenters why they experiment on animals and the answer is: "Because animals are like us." Ask the experimenters why it is morally okay to experiment on animals, and the answer is: "Because the animals are not like us." (Taylor, 2011, p. 76)

The arresting opening quotation has been retained but shortened to reflect the balance between Given and New in the paper.

The monkey's sad, scared eyes stare out at me. Its hands grip the bars of its cage. Tubes and wires from lab equipment are taped to its partly shaved skull. I came across this haunting image on the internet recently, on an animal rights site. My first instinct is to try to forget the image and think of something else. But is that responsible? As a citizen, I not only allow animals to be treated like this, but am likely to be paying for it through taxes or medical charities. In this paper, rather than avoid the uncomfortable issue being raised by animal rights campaigners, I will attempt to confront it: Is the use of animals for medical research justifiable?

The Overview's opening is vivid, informal, and personal, starting from the author's experience and dramatizing the importance of the topic.

In attempting to answer this question, the essay will consider the various arguments for and against animal experimentation in medical research as made by animal rights campaigners and medical researchers. These in turn draw on the views of scientists, philosophers, and the major world religions. I will begin by reporting the arguments against animal experimentation. In discussing both the cases against and for, I will deal with the ethical and social aspects of the case before moving to the technical ones.

This second paragraph of the Overview is more formal and sets out a map of the ground to be covered.

Note that in this version of the paper, the Against position will be considered first, an indication that it is likely to be the Given.

The ethical case against animal experimentation is based on the position that animals, particularly more intelligent animals, are similar to humans. Importantly, animals are like humans in having the capacity to feel pain. Animal experimentation requires animals to feel pain:

The opening of this paragraph reminds the reader of the map: the opening argument is about ethics.

"Animal experiments in the area of toxicology, cancer research, surgery and radiation research, amongst others, are not conceivable without considerable suffering"; in toxicology experiments, for example, "the animal is poisoned, sometimes more sometimes less quickly" (Rambeck, n.d.). As humans, we only inflict pain on other humans with their consent and for some agreed benefit. For example, doctors carry out painful operations or administer painful chemotherapy to patients in order to help them stay alive or live in less pain than before. Animal rights proponents argue that animals which are used in medical experiments, by contrast, can in no way benefit from the pain they suffer – and it is therefore unethical to inflict pain upon them. According to this view, humans who support animal experimentation are guilty of what some philosophers have described as "speciesism." Speciesism has been defined as "[b]y analogy with racism and sexism, the improper stance of refusing respect to the lives, dignity, or needs of animals of other than the human species" (Blackburn, 2005).

A technical argument made by the opponents of animal experimentation is that it is actually unhelpful. An article in the British Medical Journal, for example, reviewed several studies involving animal research and argued that there was "little evidence" to support the common assumption "that animal research has contributed to the treatment of human disease" (Pound, Ebrahim, Sandercock, Brack, & Roberts, 2004, p. 514). The same study concluded that "Even if animal experiments provide valid results and sufficiently precise estimates of treatment effects to discount the effects of chance, the extent to which the results can reasonably be generalized to humans remains open to question" (Pound et al., 2004, p. 517). This surprising conclusion may be based on the view that differences in the "anatomy, physiology and metabolism" of humans and animals make it impossible "to predict whether a human will react identically or differently based on the results of experiments conducted on animals" (Gericke, n.d.). For example, a 1983 study of carcinogenic substances conducted by the pharmaceutical company Pfizer found that "only 5–25% of the substances harmful to humans" also had adverse effects on experimental animals (Gericke, n.d.).

> The opening of this paragraph shows that we have left the ethical argument and are now moving to the first technical issue.

If it is indeed the case that the results of animal experimentation are effectively useless, this leads naturally to the third argument often made by opponents

> The opening of this paragraph signals that we are moving to the third argument against.

of animal experimentation. This argument is that the resources currently allocated to animal experimentation should instead be allocated to other medical improvement strategies such as "epidemiology, clinical research, occupational safety and health, and social medicine" (Rambeck, n.d.). A related position is that resources currently being wasted on animal experimentation should be diverted to developing hi-tech alternatives to animal testing, such as the use of human cells and tissues in combination with specialized computer programs (Gernicke, n.d.).

To summarize the case against animal experimentation, then, we can see that in the terms of the parable in the quotation with which this paper opened, opponents of animal experimentation wish to contradict both statements attributed to the experimenters. Let us note in passing that their position is in one sense similar to that of their opponents. They too wish to argue that animals are similar and dissimilar to humans. While they affirm that animals are similar to humans morally, in that both animals and humans feel pain and both have the right to avoid having pain inflicted on them against their will, opponents of animal experimentation deny the medical similarity of animals to humans. They argue instead that there is a physical dissimilarity, which means that animal experimentation is at best both useless and wasteful, and at worst, dangerously misleading.

Let us now consider the case for animal experimentation, again starting with ethics. When the experimenters argue that animals are different from humans, they are implicitly arguing that animals are not only different from humans but inferior, in some sense, to humans. This moral difference means that it is justifiable to cause suffering to animals to alleviate suffering by humans. This position is the one we have seen that animal rights advocates define as speciesism. The evidence of many human practices and institutions, such as livestock-keeping, hunting, and legal systems throughout the world, all suggest that human cultures generally have implicitly regarded human life as more important than animal life. Does such speciesism have any ethical basis? Most of the major world religions do in fact explicitly attribute more importance to human life and well-being than that of other species. Judaism, Christianity, and Islam seem to broadly agree that God has given man a unique status and authority over other beings he has created. In Hinduism and Buddhism humans are also superior to

The opening of this paragraph signals a conclusion to the first Synthesis (the Given) – the case against Animal Experimentation.

The opening sentence of this paragraph is a clear Bridge between the first Synthesis (Given) and the second Synthesis (New) – the case for animal experimentation.

The writer also reminds the reader of the map of the paper – ethical issues before technical issues.

other animals in being nearer to gods in the progress of reincarnation (Waldau, 2001, pp. 23–29). On an everyday level, it seems fair to assume that while they might not argue the case for speciesism, most human beings would demonstrate speciesism in practice. For example, if there was a choice to be made between a possibly dangerous new drug or surgical technique being tried out first on an animal before it was used on their own child, I guess that most parents would consent to the animal test, rather than, say, volunteer themselves or hire another human subject.

This leads to the technical argument of whether animal experimentation is actually useful or not. The US National Research Council points to various examples of how animal experimentation has in fact been useful. For example, the development of successful vaccines against many diseases which caused thousands of deaths in childhood at the turn of the last century – smallpox, polio, diphtheria, whooping cough – has caused them to be almost completely eradicated (National Research Council, 2004, p. 9). These vaccines all needed development and testing using animal models, as is still happening now in the development of anti-malarial vaccines. In the field of surgery, the Council also points out that heart valve replacement, organ transplants, and coronary artery bypasses are now common procedures which "would not have been possible without animal research": specifically, "the technique of sewing blood vessels together was developed through surgeries on dogs and cats" (National Research Council, 2004, p. 17). Interestingly, in light of the debate around human "speciesism," it is also pointed out by supporters that animals themselves too have benefited and will benefit from animal experimentation: for example, dogs have benefited from veterinary doctors' use of "medicines for diabetes, pacemakers for heart irregularities, hip and joint replacements for degenerative conditions, chemotherapy for cancer and vaccines against rabies" (Paul, 2002, p. 10).

This paragraph announces a transition from the ethical argument of the New section to the technical arguments.

Lastly, there is the issue of alternatives to animal experimentation. Supporters of animal experimentation "acknowledge the need for alternatives to reduce animal suffering" using criteria "often described as the three Rs of biomedical research…Reduction, Replacement, Refinement" (Murnaghan, 2010). Laws regulating the use of animals mean that ethical review panels require researchers to apply these criteria (Paul, 2002, p. 14). Refinement may involve, for example, using less invasive techniques than surgery, such as MRI scanning; such

The opening of this paragraph signals the final technical argument for the New position.

techniques may also mean there is Reduction, namely, fewer animals need to be used ("Mice, MRI's and Microchips," 2012). Suffering may also be reduced by humane attention to the animals' welfare involving both anesthesia and euthanasia where appropriate. However, Replacement is difficult to achieve because, it is argued, "animals are often the best and sometimes the only way to test the effect of medicines or other chemicals"; this is because of the difficulty of replicating the way animals "contain organs connected together in an incredibly complex system, just like humans" ("Mice, MRI's and Microchips" 2012).

To conclude this discussion of the position of animal experimentation proponents, we shall return to the parable in the opening quotation of this paper. We can now see that this position seems to be a mirror image of their opponents' position, and also draws attention to both similarity and dissimilarity. According to this position, while animals are not the same as humans, they are the most similar thing there is to us, and therefore the most safe thing on which we can possibly test new treatments and drugs. On the other hand, animals are dissimilar from humans on some moral level. If animals were not, in this moral sense, less important than humans, it would indeed be wrong to cause them to suffer on our behalf. However, there seems to be a fundamental assumption among supporters of animal experimentation that in the final analysis human life is more important than the lives of other animals. As we have seen, some animal rights supporters label supporters of animal experimentation as speciesists who refuse to respect animals' interests. I would argue that the term speciesism is itself both an ad hominem attack and an either/or fallacy: in practice, it does seem possible for humans to place animals' interests below those of humans, while at the same time respecting animals' interests, for example, by implementing ethical guidelines for animal testing such as the 3 Rs.

In conclusion, to answer the research question of this paper, *Is Animal Experimentation Justifiable?*, there seem to be two issues involved. One is whether or not animal experimentation is useful: Are animals similar enough to humans for it to be worthwhile experimenting on them? If they are not, it seems clear that animal experimentation cannot be justified. Overall, on the basis of the evidence discussed here, despite limitations on similarity, I believe the objective case for similarity

> As with the first Synthesis (Given), this paragraph wraps up the second Synthesis (New) with its own clearly signaled conclusion.

> The paper here suggests there are logical fallacies in the Given position.

> The final paragraph signals that it is a Global Conclusion to the paper, and will summarize the paper's answer to its Research Question, with its Given and New contrast.

has been made more convincingly than the case against. Animals appear to be similar enough to humans to mean that animal experimentation can be helpful in advancing human healthcare. The second issue is whether or not animal experimentation is ethical: Are animals similar enough to humans for it to be immoral to experiment on them? Or, are humans, in some essential way, superior to animals and therefore entitled to cause animals suffering in order to reduce human suffering? Any response to this second question must be subjective in that it will depend on the worldview of the individual asked. Worldviews differ on the rights and responsibilities which belong to god(s), humans, and animals. According to the worldview of this writer, haunted as I am by the thought of animals suffering, human life does take priority over animal life, and animal experimentation can, therefore, be justified.

This part of the Conclusion comes out in support of the technical arguments for the New position.

The end of the Conclusion turns to the ethical arguments. It contains a Punchline, which emphasizes the complexity of the ethical issues but comes down finally on the side of the New position.

ASSIGNMENT

Now it's time for you to write a research paper of your own. Keeping in mind the various criteria for the structure of each of the components of a research paper, and using the suggested version above as a model, write a research paper of about 2000 words.

If you want to, you could return to one of the topics raised in an earlier unit.

<h1>INDEX</h1>

agent 60

APA (documentation style) 151, 153–156, 166

appearance 8

argument ix, 64, 181–182, 189, 197, 198, 200, 201, 202; *see also* counter-argument; counter-argumentation

argumentation vii, ix, 45, 50, 101–103, 129, 136, 144

assumption ix, 1, 10, 13, 15, 18, 34, 182; *see also* given (position); given-new contrast

attribution 66-67, 69

authentic (text) vii, viii, x, 1, 66

bibliography 152, 165

body 15, 28, 34–50

brackets 100, 153, 164; *see also* citation

brainstorming 12, 148

cause-and-effect (relationship) viii, 52, 98, 111–112, 131

citation 148, 150–157, 166; *see also* brackets

claim 45, 64, 101–103, 107; *see also* argument; argumentation

components of
academic writing ix
argumentation 101
documentation 150–152
draft 183
research article 1, 13–15, 18; *see also* element

concluding statements 46, 66–69, 101; *see also* conclusion

conclusion (text structure) vii, 1, 12–15, 32, 45, 49, 50, 67, 81, 82, 86, 103–108, 129, 131, 132, 149, 168, 181–182, 186, 187, 189, 199, 201, 202; *see also* concluding statements

conclusion (logic) 129, 131, 132

conditional clauses 98–99, 138–139

conditional sentences 98, 138–139

content 63, 167

context 69

contrast 82, 103, 142; *see also* given-new contrast

counter-argument 88, 142

counter-argumentation 142–143

counter-claim 143

critique ix, 102–107

data vii, ix, 28, 32, 101, 131, 141, 149

deduction 8–9

documentation 147–166

element
of article/research paper 15, 32
of body 30
of citation 150, 153, 166
of critique 88, 105–107
of explanatory synthesis 86
of exposition 64
of expository summary 66–67
new ix, 11
see also components of

ellipsis 99–100, 174

emotion 109, 115–116, 183
end-text citation 151–152, 154, 156; *see also*
    citation
ethos 109, 114, 145
evaluation 102–107
evidence 8–9, 15, 32, 109, 149–150
explanatory synthesis 70, 81–86, 104, 177
exposition ix, 46, 50, 64, 66, 144

factual statements 46, 64–66
fallacy 109, 129, 134, 145, 201; *see also*
    logical fallacy
free-standing nouns 40

general statements 177, 183
gerunds 40–41
given (position) 32, 86, 185, 201; *see also*
    assumption; given-new contrast; new
    (position); position
given-new contrast vii, ix, 10–11, 28, 45,
    182–184
gist 3
global conclusion 103–107, 201; *see also*
    concluding statements; conclusion
global introduction 103–107, 185–186
global scene-setter 177
global statement 32

hedging 8–9
hypothetical conditional 138; *see also*
    conditional clauses; conditional
    sentences; *if* condition

if condition 37, 138; *see also* conditional
    clauses; conditional sentences;
    hypothetical conditional
in-text citation 150–156, 166; *see also*
    citation
-ing forms 40

lead summary 1, 6, 13–15, 18, 28–32, 182,
    183, 189, 197; *see also* summary
logical fallacy 109, 129–132, 134, 145, 201
logos 109, 114, 129, 145, 149

macro-structure
    of article ix, 1
    of explanatory synthesis 70, 81
modal verbs 7–9, 28
modification of position 149

navigation through text 32, 104
negative evaluation 103–108
new (position) 10–11, 13, 15, 18, 28, 32, 34,
    49, 50, 86, 102, 149, 182–187, 197, 199,
    200, 201, 202; *see also* assumption;
    given (position); given-new contrast;
    proposal (new)
nouns 40–44, 78–79, 172; *see also* noun +
    noun compounds
noun + noun compounds 43–44

outline 181–182, 184, 189
overall conclusion 82, 86
overview 1, 13, 15, 18, 28–32

paraphrase 63–64, 150
participle 40, 42
past perfect tense 27
past tense (simple) 25, 62–63
pathos 109, 114–115, 145
persuasive synthesis 88, 104, 107
plagiarism 149, 150, 152
popularized research article viii–ix, 1, 18, 34,
    147
position 13, 18, 28, 32, 86, 102, 103, 104,
    106, 107, 111, 149, 182–185, 197, 200,
    201, 202; *see also* given (position); new
    (position)
positive evaluation 102–103

premise 129, 131
present perfect tense 25–26
present tense 62
presentation
    of given/new 50, 184
    of research 1
problem-solution structure 34
problematic assumption, *see* assumption;
        see also given (position); given-new
        contrast
process (grammar) 40–41, 60
process (writing) 170, 180
pronouns
    this/that 80
    personal 113
proposal (new) 1, 34, 50
proposition 129, 140
punchline 48–51, 187, 202

questionable assumption, *see* assumption;
        see also given position
quoting 52, 63, 156

real conditionals 98–99; *see also* concitional
        clauses; conditional sentences;
        hypothetical conditional; *if* condition
reasoning 8, 114, 130, 132; *see also* fallacy;
        logical fallacy
references 145, 148, 152, 154, 155, 196; *see
        also* sources

referencing 148, 152, 153; *see also* sources
relevance, current 25, 26
reporting ix, 60, 62, 140–141
reporting verb 141
research article viii, 1, 18, 34, 87, 147

scene-setter 29, 177, 188
sources 86, 147–166*; see also* references;
        referencing
structure of
    article 18
    critique 103
    paper 183
subject (grammatical) 40, 61, 141
summary 14, 52, 64, 66–69, 81–85, 102–107,
        189
supporting details 46, 64–69, 101–102
synthesis 70, 81–85, 88, 104, 107

text organization 10, 28, 45, 63, 81, 101, 142,
        176
thesis statement 34, 66–69
title 1, 13–15, 18, 28–29, 32, 154, 156
topic ix, 11, 82, 103, 107, 150, 197
transition 82, 103–104, 142, 200

unreal conditionals 138–139

Printed in the USA
CPSIA information can be obtained
at www.ICGtesting.com
JSHW050309171223
53779JS00007B/24